Making Sparkling Wines

J. Restall & D. Hebbs

Nexus Special Interests

Nexus Special Interests Ltd
Nexus House
Boundary Way
Hemel Hempstead
Herts HP2 7ST
England

First published 1972
(Reprinted 1972, 1973, 1976, 1977, 1978, 1980, 1983)
This updated edition 1995

ISBN 1-85486-119-0

Design and typesetting by The Studio, Exeter
Printed and bound in Great Britain by Biddles Ltd, Guildford & King's Lynn

CONTENTS

ACKNOWLEDGEMENTS

We would like to thank Mr. G. M. Young of Moussec Limited, Rickmansworth, for his valued advice and assistance on technical aspects, and also Mr. Derek Baldwin, Twickenham, for providing excellent line illustrations and photographs along with his wife, Mary, who coped with the bulk of the typing as well as making many useful suggestions to improve the quality of the manuscript. Finally, may we thank our wives, Doris and Rona, for their patience in gracefully accepting a temporary loss of our company and conversation.

Photographs of the Champagne by courtesy of the C.I.V.C. Epernay, kindly arranged by Col. Maurice Buckmaster.

DEDICATION

This book is dedicated to wine yeast and to the many friends made possible by its existence. We thank them for helpful suggestions and ideas incorporated in our manuscript.

FOREWORD

Most of us have at some time or another fallen under the spell and fascination of sparkling wines. Many of us, too, have often wished that we could produce high quality sparkling wines with the same regularity and certainty that we can produce ordinary still wines. Occasionally, of course, the winemaker is delighted when he finds that a wine which he thought to be still, pétillant or even sparkling, and when this occurs in a wine of the right type it is an event to be welcomed. On such occasions the thought crosses the winemaker's mind: how wonderful it would be if I could do this whenever I wished!

That is the purpose of this book. "Accidental" sparkling wines, delightful as they may be, have nothing of the superb quality that can be found in a wine which has been designed, made and matured as such according to the basic principles of sparkling wine production. John Restall and Don Hebbs have made a long study of the continental methods of producing sparkling wines, and have carried out many years' experiments in order to be able to write this book into which they have distilled—if that is the word!—their accumulated and joint experience.

The emphasis throughout is on *quality,* for, as they rightly point out in many places, sparkling wines of quality are rarely made accidentally or quickly; they can only be made if the correct basic processes are employed, and adequate maturation is given. *Quality* sparkling wine can certainly be produced by the amateur and this book will give you all the background knowledge you require and explain in detail the methods you should employ to produce the most impressive and delicious sparkling wines.

I state that with certainty, for I have tasted the delightful sparkling wines which the two authors have produced and which I venture to say would stand comparison with many of the champagnes to be found on commercial shelves. The authors are too modest to say so, so I will say it for them!

I am sure that this book will be greatly welcomed by thousands of winemakers, both beginners and experienced, and is a worthy addition to the ever growing library of amateur winemaking literature.

And to celebrate the event, what better than a bottle of SPARKLING WINE!

CYRIL BERRY

CHAPTER 1

Why Make Sparkling Wines?

Sparkling wines....! What is their fascination? Why are they so popular? There is no doubt at all that a sparkling wine has "that little something that the others haven't got"—the pop of the cork, the gush of foam, the lively bubbles dancing upward in the glass—all delight the eye with the promise of pleasure to come. Is it surprising that sparkling wines are unsurpassed for creating a festive atmosphere, and for making any party go with a swing?

There are many commercial sparkling wines and the queen of them all, of course, is Champagne. Champagne...what magic there is in the word! The mere mention of it brings to the mind a whole string of happy associations—gay parties, celebrations, wedding breakfasts, Edwardian toasts from actresses' slippers, popping corks, and romance — and there is no doubt that champagne has established this "image" in the public mind. But there are many other admirable sparkling drinks — the Italian Asti Spumante, the German Sekt, the Portuguese Mateus Rosé, the Burgundian mousseux, or the Spanish Cava — and, inevitably, any winemaker who can produce good table wines will eventually be tempted to try making sparkling wine of his own.

To be able to produce for your guests a bottle of your own "bubbly" marks you out as a winemaker of real distinction, and your visitors cannot fail to be impressed.

And it is not really difficult, although one does need to take some pains. Apart from collecting some sound empty champagne bottles, the additional gear required is easily knocked-up and will not prove expensive. The process requires the fermentation to be concluded in a corked bottle, so that the carbon dioxide gas generated in the conversion of the final priming sugar into alcohol dissolves in the wine. Considerable pressure is built up as the gas accumulates and when the bottle is uncorked the gas comes out of solution to produce the well known champagne effect.

Strong bottles and special corks must be used and the latter have to be wired in position. Because this secondary fermentation is completed in the bottle there will inevitably be some *lees,* or sediment, in the bottle afterwards. This has to be removed, to clear the wine, and at the same time sufficient sugar must be added to provide an adequate sparkle in the wine without generating too much pressure. These are the two main problems facing the sparkling winemaker. The pressure for champagne is from 75 to 90 p.s.i., but we prefer to work at a considerably lower pressure, to be on the safe side, especially as used champagne bottles have to be employed.

It must be pointed out that bottles under pressure should be handled carefully at all times and that the recommendations we make concerning sugar additions should on no accout be exceeded, otherwise an excessive gas pressure will be generated and might prove dangerous. An exploding bottle can cause injury.

We have dealt with our subject in an entirely practical manner and have not made statements that we cannot qualify and have *not* delved into the realms of applied chemistry relating to wine making, for that has already been covered more than adequately in other publications by specialists in the field. Familiarity with certain winemaking and technical terms is desirable, but to fully understand the complexity of chemical formulae and reaction is unnecessary, in our opinion, when considering the relatively small scale of wine production in which most of us are likely to be engaged.

In writing this book, we have certainly increased our background knowledge by sharing one another's ideas and experience on the subject. We now hope that we can encourage our fellow winemakers to make their own sparkling wine, and they can if they follow the methods and techniques we describe. Some of the techniques are relatively simple; others are more complex. The simple methods call for careful decanting to avoid disturbing the yeast sediment left in the bottle. The more complex techniques require greater effort and expertise to produce a sparkling wine which has every chance of being comparable to the one purchased from the local wine merchant.

We do not expect the absolute beginner to plunge into sparkling winemaking; in fact, it is desirable to have a fair basic knowledge of general principles and some practical experience before he attempts to put that delightful sparkle into his wines. We have been at pains to stress certain factors which are important both for quality and for safety, but much of what we say applies equally well to ordinary table wine production.

Commercial champagne and sparkling wines are generally made from the grape. The amateur may well follow this procedure, either by using fresh grapes or grape juice concentrate. On the other hand, he may feel inclined to use other fruits such as apples, apricots, gooseberries, or strawberries, to mention but a few. The fruit flavour, providing that it is not overpowering, will produce what can only be described as a delightful sparkling wine.

We thought it useful to provide an account of the commercial procedures for champagne and other sparkling wines made in different parts of the world. As grape growers and amateur sparkling winemakers for a number of years, we naturally regard commercial techniques from a more practical view-point than do some profesional authors on the subject. They usually write for the layman or the wine-trade, but we have had in mind the chap whose hobby is winemaking.

Here's a toast to your success - in sparkling wine, naturally!

CHAPTER 2

Champagne

When we are discussing sparkling wines we surely must not neglect to make a reasonably close study of the greatest of them all — champagne.

Champagne needs no advertisement, for it has come to epitomise quality and luxury. Men write songs about it, girls go giggly under its influence, and ships are launched with its blessing. Some rave about champagne, and some say it is over-rated, but the fact remains that it has come to be regarded as the universal symbol of success, prosperity, quality and happiness.

Champagne has many uses; its stimulating qualities as an aperitif are noteworthy and it has the advantage, like rosé, that people who cannot make up their own minds what wine to choose can drink it throughout the meal. (We ourselves feel that other wines may often be far more appropriate to a particular course). And as a morale-booster it is without equal!

How many who celebrate fully appreciate and savour the magnificence of the bouquet of a vintage champagne, and the delicate, fresh taste of the grapes from which it was originally made? By tradition, the wine is made predominantly from the juice of red grapes; the reason may have faded into obscurity, but the subtle bequest in character from these red grapes, is thought to be significant. Good champagne has an unrivalled richness, despite the fact that it may be completely dry; there is no need to hide any imperfections behind a veil of sugar.

The Champagne Country, strictly limited in area by French law, is centred around the two noteworthy towns of Rheims and Épernay which lie to the east of Paris and may be reached in only half a day by road from Calais.

The tourist may well feel that the vineyards of the Valley of the Marne are typical of the Champagne area as a whole. He would be quite wrong, for this is the only road (the N3 connecting Paris and Epernay) which gives a good view of vineyards. These vineyards, however, do not generally have a high rating for quality, especially at the far end of the valley. The high category vineyards of the Champagne region are invariably tucked away well off the beaten track, and to be seen to advantage require a diversion from the main highways. The discoveries to be made are amply rewarding.

If you break your journey, on the return to a channel port from a sunshine holiday in the south, the large champagne concerns, or "houses", as they are called in Rheims and Epernay, will welcome you cordially, and you will be shown true *Champenois* hospitality. This usually includes an extensive conducted tour of the underground cellars hewn in the chalk, complemented by a most enjoyable tasting session. Some of these cellars are in "storeys", four deep, and cover many miles.

How it all began

Up to the end of the seventeenth century all the wine made in the region was still, some was whitish in colour, but the majority had a reddish hue. The wine was made by the traditional method of pressing the grapes, to be followed by a natural fermentation of the grape juice into wine. This was stored in wooden casks until ready to drink. In the springtime, the wine often became fretful (unstable). The region is considerably further north than the other important grape growing areas of France and with a poor year — little sunshine to fully ripen the grapes — and when the harvest was necessarily late, the onset of the winter often terminated the fermentation long before all the sugar had been fermented out. The advent of spring and the consequent rise in temperature often revived the dormant yeast cells into activity to work on the remaining sugar. The result would have been a *pétillant* wine which is prickly on the palate as it is charged with carbon dioxide gas. As amateur winemakers, most of us will have experienced this effect at some time or other, and no doubt the occurrence has not always been intentional or welcomed. In those days, the importance of repeated racking from the yeast sediment

5

in producing still wines had not been realised.

It was Dom Pérignon, a Benedictine monk, the cellar master of a monastery on the Mountain of Rheims, called Hautvillers, who reputedly first grasped the true significance of this. Some twenty years elapsed before he finally achieved his ambition and, about 1690, produced a saleable sparkling wine. This wine almost certainly would not have been anything like as lively as the champagne of today. No additional sugar would have been added and in any case bottles such as were manufactured in those days would not have withstood gas pressures such as those with which we are now familiar.

In Dom Pérignon's day wine was taken straight from the cask to the table. The bottles available at that time were expensive and stoppers rather crude, they were made from wood bound with hemp. Corks as we know them did not exist. It is thought that Dom Pérignon encouraged the glass workers of the day to make for him special bottles of sufficient strength to cope with his early champagne. Legend has it that he first became aware of the possibilities of natural cork as a stopper material when two monks travelling from Spain to Sweden broke their journey at Hautvillers. He observed with considerable interest that their water containers were fitted with Spanish corks of much the same form as are now generally used for still wines. With corks from the Costa Brava and with improved bottles, he was able to seal off the gas pressure and conserve the natural sparkle in the wine. He had thus paved the way for the emergence of champagne as a wine with a world wide reputation and demand. This embryonic champagne is believed to have been served from frosted glasses, for at that time methods of removing the cloudiness and yeast sediment had not been devised, and few people relish the sight of a cloudy wine. The processes of *remuage* (settling the yeast on to the cork) and *dégorgement* (disgorging), to produce a crystal-clear champagne, were later innovations and credit for them has been given to the widow Cliquot of the old-established house of Veuve Cliquot-Ponsardin. Legend has it that she was the widow of a vineyard owner in days following the time of Dom Pérignon. In pondering on the problem, it occurred to her that if the bottles were inverted the sediment would settle out on the corks; so she had a number of holes bored in a table to accommodate the bottles for this very purpose. Refinements followed, with the tables being stood against the wall to save space and at the same time the holes were made oval in shape, so that the bottle positions could, over a period of time with repeated twisting, be moved from an oblique angle to a vertical position. This procedure was found to further accelerate the settling of the yeast. The process was termed *remuage* (twisting, or agitating) and the tables were later hinged together to provide access to both sides and they were christened *pupitres,* or desks. Exactly the same process is used today, in the cellars beneath Rheims and Épernay.

The Grapes

French law dictates that champagne may only be made from four species of grape, the Pinot, the Chardonnay, the Arbanne and the Petit Meslier (less than 1% of the total cultivation is devoted to the two latter vines). Harvesting normally begins in late September, but may in a poor year run well into October.

The Pinot, a red species, is considered an aristocrat amongst vines and although a shy bearer it yields an extremely high quality delicate wine, rich in bouquet. The varieties of the Pinot are numerous, but the Noir and the Meunier are the most common. The Chardonnay, a white grape, on the other hand is a more prolific bearer. Classic champagne is invariably made from the juice of three parts of Pinot to one of Chardonnay.

Only 14% of the vineyards are owned by the large "Houses," the balance being in the hands of a great number of private vignerons who have always been reluctant to dispose of their property. Over the years, larger vineyards have been divided up within the family on the decease of the owner. Some of the vineyards are quite small and many are managed as a side-line activity. However, there are some co-operatives of a considerable acreage.

The greater part of the harvest is purchased by the well-known shippers, and the task of the vine grower normally ends on delivery of the grapes to the press.

Soil

The vineyards normally have a limestone base, and the consequent chalky subsoil assures good drainage, but sufficient humidity is retained for the vines. It is thought that the delicacy of the wine is influenced by

7

the chalk, the grapes from the hill vines are superior to those grown on the alluvial soil of the valleys.

Climate

The climate of the Champagne is similar to that of Paris — winter is generally mild, spring variable, summer hot, and autumn relatively fine. The average annual temperature is only 10°C (50°F). This is the limit for the European wine belt not so much for the life of the vine, but for maturation of the grapes.

Pressing

The hydraulic presses of the Champagne are massive, and the *maie* (cage) is shallow and of large diameter — some 10 feet across. This unique design permits the rapid removal of the juice, with minimum of pressure, to ensure that there is little tainting of the colourless juice by the pigment of the red skins. The *maie* will take some 4000 kilos (approximately 4 tons) of grapes, but only some 2660 litres from this *marc* may be used for champagne. The balance is made into *vin ordinaire* for local consumption. The pressing is carried out quickly, in several stages, and each stage is punctuated by raising the *mouton* (pressure pad) so that the compressed grapes may be turned over with wooden spades to facilitate extraction. Many new techniques for juice extraction are now replacing old traditional methods.

Débourbage ("purging" or sulphiting of the must)

The juice from the press is either run into an open vat or a specially lined concrete tank situated below the level of the press-house and sulphur dioxide gas is introduced to temporarily inhibit the yeast action, so that the debris comprising torn grapes, stalks and vineyard dust, may settle out to provide a clean *must*.

To ferment on this debris would have an adverse effect upon the quality of the wine and would not support the high standard quality expected of a champagne. If more amateur winemakers practised *débourbage* in the formulation of their still white wines, quality would no doubt, benefit enormously.

The First Fermentation

This clean *must* is either transferred from the settling tank to oak-casks or large fermentation vats. There has been a definite swing towards the use of stainless steel or plastic lined fermentation vats in recent times, and eventually oak casks are expected to be replaced by vats, especially as champagne gains no real benefit from storage in wood; it is the time spent in the bottle which is most rewarding. Some of the modern vats have a storage capacity of 33,000 litres and provision for artificial cooling is made to control the rise in temperature due to the fermentation of such a large volume. For the fermentation, the *champenois* vintners sometimes rely upon natural yeasts indigenous to the area, but when weather conditions have been unfavourable prior to the harvest, a yeast starter from a cultured strain is employed. In order to produce the perfect wine, control over temperature is essential and 15°C. (60°F) is aimed at to provide the optimum conditions for a slow steady fermentation. Where casks are used, artificial heat has often to be provided, especially at the end of the fermentation which should finish with not more than 2 gms. of sugar per litre. The temperature of the fermenting wine in the large vats is controlled by stainless steel cooling coils. Fermentation is normally complete in two or three weeks, but under some conditions can carry on for a longer period. When all the casked wines have fermented out the cellar doors are opened to admit the cold air to assist in the settling of the suspended yeasts and other foreign matter in the wine prior to the first racking.

Racking is the name given to the process of removing the wine from its sediment and the first racking may be carried out in November, but exactly when it is done depends much upon the time of harvest. In transferring to the new container the wine is normally aerated by splashing it into an intermediate vessel. The sediment from the first racking can be as much as 4% of the total volume and is usually sold to be distilled into a rough brandy.

The cold weather hastens the drop out of tartrates and other foreign matter, the second racking usually takes place during mid-December. A continuous check is kept on the wine which is assessed for flavour and tested in the laboratory for acid content and any bacterial infection. The sulphur dioxide content is carefully controlled at a low level.

Following the first racking most of the *champenois* vintners, who ferment their wines in casks, assemble wines from different vineyards, but where large capacity vats are used this assemblage would have already been carried out before the *musts* were actually transferred.

The Preparation of the Cuvée

During the five week period embracing Christmas, January and early February the wine is allowed to rest and during this time there will be a further fall-out of suspended foreign matter.

Throughout this five week period the most difficult and exacting phase of the *méthod champenoise* takes place. It is then that a selection of young and rather harsh still wines has to be made to compose the blend required for the bottle fermentation. This is known as the *Cuvée*. The responsibility for the decisions made falls upon the *chef de cave,* who may well be the owner of the company. Just how difficult this task is can be realised from the fact that the young wines being blended at this time taste nothing like the finished product, yet they have some years hence to produce a champagne, consistent in quality and character with that of previous years.

It is of course desirable to complete the blending process before the cold weather ceases, for when different wines are mixed together instability may ensue and promote cloudiness, despite the fact that the original wines may have been quite clear. Cold conditions are useful here.

We have referred to the *cuvée* in the singular, but the large "houses" (Bollinger, Heidsieck, Krug, to mention but a few) will in fact have more than one line running through the cellars. There may be a vintage being produced along with the non-vintage champagnes. A certain proportion of the still wine is always stored in the cellars for future use. Some of the previous year's reserve wine may well be contained in the *cuvées* of the current year.

Fining

Prior to bottling, the wines are usually fined. Complete limpidity is sometimes induced by the addition of isinglass to the wine and in a poor year gelatine and additional tannin will be required to provide the requisite clarity, but these days Bentonite and pressure filtering would be employed. Then an additional racking is carried out to lift the clear wine from the sediment so formed. It would be pointless to bottle a cloudy wine in the hope that it might clear eventually, because once bottled, there is no way of clearing easily.

The Second Fermentation

In early April the first of the blended wine is transferred to an extremely large vat, frequently of a capacity of 400 hectolitres (8,800 gallons). It is then that the additional sugar, known as the *liqueur de tirage,* required for the second fermentation is added. The wine needs to contain 10% to 11.5% of alcohol and sufficient sugar is added to provide a total of 24 gm. per litre (4 oz. per gallon) — there may well be a trace of sugar already present. This quantity of sugar will provide what is considered by commercial standards as safe working pressure (75-90 p.s.i.) of carbon dioxide gas and will generally raise the alcohol content by 1.2% to finally take the wine out to dryness in the subsequent fermentation which takes place in the corked bottle. A champagne yeast will generally terminate its activity at about 13.8% alcohol. This can cause problems in a particularly good year, such as 1959, when some of the still wine contains as much as 14% alcohol. Unless this wine is blended with one of lower alcoholic content, from a previous year, there will be no effervescence from the bottles, so it is not unknown for vintage champagnes to be degraded (to some extent) by the addition of low alcohol wines, in order to achieve a satisfactory bottle fermentation.

The yeast starter added to the wine is generally prepared from a special culture (yeast grown in a laboratory), but may be obtained from the owner's own grapes, or from the sediment of a previous year's bottle. This *seeded* wine may well be allowed to begin fermenting before being bottled. It would certainly be checked in the laboratory for soundness.

Bottling

This generally extends through April, May and June, and these days all but the smallest concerns use mechanical bottling plants. The operation is usually carried out above ground. The cork, which is double the size of the diameter of the bottle neck, is fitted and secured by an *agrafe* shaped like an inverted U which the machine bends under the rim to provide secure fitting until removed at the *dégorgement* stage. Today, many shippers have gone over to the use of crown corks, of similar design to the closures used on mineral water and beer bottles. This latter method is quicker in operation, much cheaper, and avoids the danger of the champagne becoming *corked*.

Cellaring

In the large concerns the bottles are transferred to the cellars on a conveyor-belt system. The higher quality champagnes are invariably stored in the deepest cellars, where they undergo the second fermentation between 10°C. (50°F.) and 12°C. (54°F.) Such temperatures ensure the slow fermentation associated with high quality, and this normally lasts between two and three months. As amateur sparkling winemakers, we would indeed be hard pressed to find such conditions for the storage of our own sparkling wines, but if we are realistic we may admit that we are not likely to achieve the degree of excellence expected of a vintage champagne. Furthermore, it is unlikely that our palates will have received the expensive education which is necessary for a full appreciation of such a wine. These conditions of storage are considered to provide a finer and more persistent bouquet and also to make the subsequent operation of *remuage* that much easier to perform.

The bottles are stacked, in the horizontal position with unbelievable precision, in neat rows throughout the galleries composing the extensive underground network of passages hewn in the chalk. During the second fermentation the alcoholic content will be increased by approximately 1.2% and the carbon dioxide gas generated, being unable to escape, has no alternative but to go into solution in the wine. This will, in fact, produce a pressure of something like 90 p.s.i.

The yeast sediment will eventually settle in a line along the side of the bottle. A constant check is always kept on sample bottles by inserting a hypodermic needle connected to a pressure gauge and should the second fermentation be considered to be sluggish, the bottle will be moved to warmer surroundings. There will inevitably be some breakages; however these days, with careful laboratory control over the process, not more than 0.5% of the champagne would be expected to be lost. In Victorian times it was not unusual for the losses to be as much as 50% of the vintage!

Ageing

Champagne does not attain perfection overnight; French law dictates that non-vintage champagne is required to spend at least one year on the yeast deposit. Vintage champagne cannot be sold until three years have elapsed since the date of the harvest. In practice, the non-vintages are invariably older than one year and the vintages will not be released until four or five years have passed since the grapes were originally harvested. It is unusual to find more than one vintage offered for sale at any particular time. Champagne is normally left on its yeast sediment until near the time expected for shipment. This is more convenient for storage and also is of advantage in proving greater maturity. During the ageing period complex chemical changes take place, the acids react with the alcohol to form esters and reduce the level of the former to some extent. The prolonged exposure of the wine to the yeast sediment, which is allied to amino-acids, reinforces the development of the bouquet produced by ester formation. A once harsh wine takes on an air of smoothness to become mature, well-balanced and radiant with bouquet.

The bottles are periodically restacked to remove the broken ones and a few with weeping corks. The contents of the latter are combined with a fermenting wine and eventually find their way back again to the ageing process. During the re-stacking the bottles are "roused" (shaken up) to disperse the sediment, in order to provide homogeneity by breaking up the strata of dead or inactive yeast cells and tartrates.

Remuage (twisting, or agitating)

Once the wine is sufficiently mature, the process of settling the sediment on to the stoppers, *remuage*, is begun. In the vernacular, *remuage* is pronounced rer'mu'arge. The bottles destined for this process are placed in *pupitres* (or desks) which stand nearly five feet

13

high and each contain some 120 standard sized champagne bottles. The process usually takes about two months to complete and every other day, at least at the beginning of the process, a *remueur* will give each bottle a skilful twist, rotating them one-eighth of a turn. During this period the bottles, which were originally at an angle of 45°, will gradually be brought up into a vertical position (still upside down). The twisting action dislodges the sediment from the glass, so that it gradually settles on the stopper. The technique requires considerable skill which is only achieved by practical experience and despite innovations to simplify the process, no entirely satisfactory alternative has yet been found. The amateur winemaker is unlikely to be able to perform this function with ease of the French *remueur* but we have alternatives to *remuage* and *dégorgement* which provide a perfectly limpid sparkling wine for show purposes. We describe the method in Chapter 12.

Dégorgement

"Disgorging" is the name given to the process for removing the sediment which has been encouraged to settle firmly on the stoppers during remuage.

In the classic method the bottle was held, still in the upside-down position, and whilst retaining the cork with the index finger the string was cut. At the precise second when the pressure was felt to be forcing the cork out, the bottle was thrust away from the body by a swift movement, so that the cork was pointing upwards at an angle of about 30°.

This swinging thrust had the effect of causing the air bubble in the bottle to fly up into the neck, where it acted as a cushion, when both sediment and cork flew out, to reduce the loss of the contents. To prevent an effervescent overspill a thumb was then placed over the opening until a new cork was fitted. This process is known as *dégorgement a la volée*.

Needless to say, this sequence of operations required considerable practice to develop the skill required to achieve success every time. The worker concerned is known as a *dégorgeur*.

Today, this process has been simplified by immersing the necks of the inverted bottles in a freezing mixture, so that the yeast deposit is held firm in a frozen slug of ice. When sufficient ice has formed in the neck to encapsulate the yeast the bottle is turned and a wire fixing or special clamp called an agrafe is removed to let the yeast-loaded ice slug fly out, before fitting the final cork; this process is known as *dégorgement à la glacé.*

The old method is still used where small batches are being processed, but by far the greater part of champagne disgorging these days is carried out mechanically. The bottles are transported on a conveyor system, upside down, to pass the necks through a freezing trough to encapsulate the sediment in the ice formed in the bottle necks. Automatic machines remove the stoppers from the bottles, to free the imprisoned yeast sediment, before adding the topping up liquid, known as the *liqueur d'expédition,* to provide the degree of sweetness to suit the market concerned. The *liqueur d'expédition* contains pure cane sugar dissolved in wine to which may be added some spirit; the process is known as *dosage.* Finally the new corks will be machine fitted and secured by the wire *muselets* (muzzles). The bottles, dressed with the characteristic foil wrapping, will then be labelled. The presence of the foil is traditional and although thought to hide the variation in the vacant space beneath the cork, the original reason was more probably to prevent mice from gnawing away at the string retaining the corks, when the bottles were stored in the cellars. In the early days of champagne wire was not available for this purpose.

Sweetness in Champagne

Surprisingly enough, the average Frenchman prefers his champagne sweet, for when he drinks champagne with a meal it invariably complements the dessert course. It was the English, many years ago, who first insisted upon dry champagne. This requirement was not exactly welcomed by the *champenois* vintners as they could no longer conceal imperfections and an excess of acid with the *liqueur d'expédition.* This country is still the principal importer of champagne, but now only leads the United States by a narrow margin. It is said that only a very old champagne may be appreciated to perfection when completely dry and invariably a Brut (very dry) champagne will contain a trace of sugar to temper the edge of dryness.

We find that we can produce a similar dry sparkling wine, which has popular appeal (not champagne, of course!) by adding small amounts of glycerine to the *cuvée* prior to the second fermentation. This will temper the edge of dryness and remove the necessity of adding duty-laden spirit to stabilise the cane sugar, a precaution which would normally be required.

The degrees of dryness or sweetness commonly encountered are:

Brut, Nature, Dry	*Very dry*
Extra-sec	*Dry*
Sec or Gout Americain	*Slightly sweet*
Demi-sec or Gout Francais	*Sweet*
Mi-doux or Demi-doux	*Very sweet*
Doux	*Exceptionally sweet*

Prior to shipment, the bottles will be allowed to rest for approximately six months to recover from the rigours of *dégorgement* and *dosage*. Some firms may post-store their champagne for as long as one year, especially if they are dry.

Imperfections in the technique and the quality of the grapes used for any dry wines are difficult to hide from a discerning palate.

VINTAGE CHAMPAGNE is the product of a blend of wines forming the *cuvée* from a single year, when the weather conditions have been particularly favourable so that the grapes ripened to perfection. Such a champagne specifies the year of the harvest on the label and is of superlative quality.

NON-VINTAGE CHAMPAGNE is produced from years when the sun has not been so forthcoming. In fact the *cuvée* for a non-vintage may contain still wines from other years and will certainly include some wines from a vintage year. Each year a proportion of the harvest is destined to be stored in the cellars, so that whatever the season has been, there is always wine to fall back on for the production of a *cuvée*. The quality of a non-vintage is not so very far removed from that of the vintage and would be eminently suitable for formal occasions where the guests are more interested in what is going on than in the champagne. Vintage champagne would generally be wasted at such a gathering and would be more appropriate to the intimate occasions where the wine is *tasted* rather than merely drunk. A similar philosophy may be adopted when serving one's own treasured and prized sparkling wine.

BLANC DE BLANCS. The *cuvée* of classical champagne is derived from a blend of the juice of white and red grapes, but some champagne is made only from the juice of white grapes and this is advertised as being somewhat lighter in texture, but its novelty value appears to attract a higher price. We have yet to hear anyone complain that traditional champagne is too heavy!

BUYER'S OWN BRAND is always recommended for parties and is unlikely to be as wonderful as a champagne bearing the shipper's name on the label — it is normally sold under the retailer's own brand name. When a discerning guest is expected there could of course be a more expensive bottle in the background!

Authors' Note: Readers seeking a more comprehensive knowledge of the subject, are advised to refer to Patric Forbes' *Champagne,* published by Victor Gollancz, a standard text book on the subject.

CHAPTER 3

Other Sparkling Wines

The *méthode champenoise* calls for the secondary fermentation to be carried out in the bottle, but in many of the other wine producing regions of the world, as well as France, a vast amount of sparkling wine is made by the *cuve close* method (also known as the tank or Charmat process) which is nothing like as laborious. The second fermentation is conducted in a pressurised vitreous enamelled or stainless-steel tank, from which the wine is simply filtered and bottled and of course the tedious procedures applicable to removing the yeast sediment from individual bottles are no longer necesssary.

Sparkling wine made this way foams quite well in the glass, but does not retain its sparkle for as long as wine made by the classic method. It is, however, a sensible way to make a cheaper sparkling wine. In the other wine producing regions of France sparkling wines made by both methods are called *vins mousseux*. The *méthode champenoise* is, however, not entirely restricted to the Champagne region and is in fact used in many wine producing countries to provide the best quality, and necessarily more expensive sparkling wines. Invariably the names *cuve close* and *méthod champenoise* will appear on the labels of these sparkling wines. A simple carbonated wine, on the other hand, which froths for a moment and then becomes flat rather quickly, would not be entitled to either of these qualifications.

FRANCE. There is hardly a wine producing district in France which does not make a sparkling wine of some kind, but it has been said that a good deal of them have been given a sparkle in order to make an indifferent wine marketable, rather than to emphasise the innate qualities of the best wine that can be made in the particular area, as is the case with Champagne.

THE LOIRE. It would be true to say that the best of the other sparkling wines originate from the Loire Valley, and of these a sparkling **Vouvray** would be considered to be a little richer and more full bodied than a champagne. The flavour of the grapes is more pronounced and the dry **Vouvray** would be sweeter than its champagne counterpart. **Samur** is also well known for producing sparkling wines, the particular one that comes to mind is the medium sweet Golden Guinea, which has a hint of the muscat flavour and has been marketed in this country for a number of years.

BURGUNDY is another notable region where a good deal of sparkling wine is produced and, of course, is well known for the red sparkling Burgundy whose bubbles burst to make a rather annoying multitude of tiny red stains, which contrast rather well against a white shirt! The best of the sparkling Burgundies, according to Hugh Johnson, is the pink one known as *Oeil de Perdrix* — partridge eye. Those white sparkling Burgundies, made by the *méthode champenoise,* are said to have little resemblance to the white still wine of origin. Of course it would be most unlikely, if not unthinkable, for a quality white burgundy to be given a sparkle.

BORDEAUX produces some very pleasant white sparkling wine mainly by the *cuve close* method, but this is not always indicated on the label. Veuve du Vernay has become so popular in this country that it now offers serious competition to classic champagne.

A rather delicate medium sweet sparkling wine is made at **Limoux** near Carcassone and considerably further away, more robust sparkling wines as one would expect, are produced in the **Rhône Valley** region; but strangely enough, one of them from **Seyssel** is so delicate that it is said to be easily confused with champagne. However, the best known sparking wine of the Rhône made by the *méthod champenoise* comes from **Saint-Pèray,** the oldest vineyard of the region.

GERMANY. The Germans really go for sparkling wine in a big way and the industry connected with their sparkling wine, called Sekt, is of comparable size to the champagne industry of France.

It is interesting to note that a good deal of sparkling fruit wine is made commercially in Germany and the demand for sparkling strawberry is such that they have had to import this fruit recently, in order to satisfy the colossal demand.

Although the best of the German Sekts are comparable to the French champagnes, a good deal of wine which is difficult to market is given a sparkle. This is not an invitation to amateur winemakers to "fizz-up" their own also-rans, for the painstaking effort required in the processing would be worthy of greater potential.

ITALY is best known for Asti-Spumante which is made from the muscat grape, takes its name from the town of Asti near Turin, and is manufactured by the well known firms of Martini, Gancia and Cinzano. This wine is very popular in this country, but even the dry version is very far from being dry to an educated palate. In fact it has been suggested that Asti-Spumante is served to a much better advantage when considerably colder than would be normal for a champagne.

SPAIN. Most of the Spanish sparkling wine, Cava, is produced in Catalonia and is practically all made by the *méthod champenoise*. The cellars, where Codorniu is produced, are said to be the largest in Europe. As well as being one of the major grape-based sparkling wine producers, Spain makes a considerable amount of sparkling wine from apples in the northern regions; they call it "Sidra." In fact it is not unlike the cheaper grape-based sparkling wines, and certainly indicates that the apple is good material for our purpose.

CALIFORNIA produces some really excellent sparkling wine from the Vitis Vinifera grapes (of European origin) which they actually call "champagne". Were it not of such good quality the French would probably be less concerned! The Americans use the *méthod champenoise* extensively and are not shy in labelling the process.

NEW YORK STATE. The sparkling wines of New York State are reputed to make wonderful aperitifs, but the wine made from the indigenous grapes of the North American continent have an unusual flavour and unless both the grape juice and wine is specially treated, the wine has what may be called an "acquired taste" by some Vitis Vinifera wine lovers.

MOUSSEC of Rickmansworth in Hertfordshire have been making a sparkling wine from grape juice concentrate since 1930. In those early days the wine was actually made by the *méthod champenoise* (some of the original pupitres still exist), but now both their dry and sweet sparkling wines are produced from the *cuve close* method exclusively from concentrate grape juice which is mainly processed at their own plant, situated in the Aube, a department of the province of Champagne. Moussec is much better value for money, in our opinion, than many of the cheaper imported sparkling wines.

20

MERRYDOWN in Sussex have been making fruit wines since 1947 and are well known not only for their first venture, apple wine, but for a range of other country wines. In recent years the demand has encouraged the company to launch out with both sparkling apple and strawberry, made entirely from fresh fruit by the *cuve close* method. These sparkling wines are most attractive in both price and quality.

Flow Chart

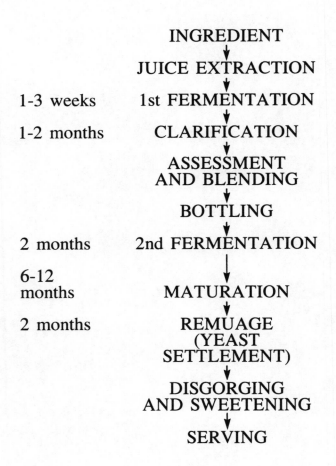

	INGREDIENT
	↓
	JUICE EXTRACTION
	↓
1-3 weeks	1st FERMENTATION
	↓
1-2 months	CLARIFICATION
	↓
	ASSESSMENT AND BLENDING
	↓
	BOTTLING
	↓
2 months	2nd FERMENTATION
	↓
6-12 months	MATURATION
	↓
2 months	REMUAGE (YEAST SETTLEMENT)
	↓
	DISGORGING AND SWEETENING
	↓
	SERVING

Authors' note: Where an exploratory tasting or early usage is desired the maturation period may be curtailed or even omitted.

CHAPTER 4

Bottles and Closures

As will become clear later, because of the high pressures involved, only true champagne bottles should be used for making sparkling wine, and care should be taken to see that they are in sound condition.

When a large number of used champagne bottles is required the best time for the search is in May or June, a time of the year popular for wedding receptions; but at many hotels, particularly in the larger cities, supplies are available practically all the year round. An enthusiastic sparkling-wine producing colleague of ours could have completely filled the boot of his car from a recent visit made to a well known hotel in Park Lane, London.

It is always a good idea to cultivate the acquaintance of the head wine waiter or his assistant, so that the used champagne bottles may be put aside specially; bottles which have remained empty for a considerable time tend to develop mould growth and uninviting scents, and are consequently difficult to clean.

Any bottles which are badly scratched or pitted should be discarded, for they will be weak in the vicinity of the damage and may be prone to fracture under pressure. New champagne bottles intended for commercial use, whether empty or filled, are cherished with every care; but once empty an entirely different attitude is adopted, so beware of the scars of rough handling. Commercial sparkling wine bottles should be avoided - go for the much heavier true champagne ones.

Removing Labels

We always remove the original shipper's labels from the bottles; the new occupant should be able to stand on its own reputation! We have found that the more expensive the champagne the more difficult it is to remove the labels. Obviously, the shipper does not want his labels to become detached in the ice-bucket and his wine to lose its identity, so he uses a water-resistant gum; but all labels appear to yield to soaking in warm water. The remaining decorative foil frequently provides a more tedious problem and often requires careful scraping to effect its complete removal.

Cleaning Bottles

Bottles must be scrupulously clean inside to avoid contamination and to facilitate the removal of the yeast deposit during *remuage*. We favour the use of domestic bleach (sodium hypochlorite), as this not only has a sterilising action, but also removes adherent deposits from dirty bottles. Sulphite solution has no cleaning properties. However, bleach contains free sodium hydroxide (caustic soda), which will attack glass, so it should not be permitted to remain in the bottles for prolonged periods, or the action of this free sodium hydroxide may roughen the inside surface of the bottle and make it harder to shake down the yeast.

Detergents such as "Silana P.F." can be used to advantage, but whatever method is employed the bottles must be thoroughly rinsed to remove the last traces of the cleaning agent. The presence of even small traces of detergent can be ruinous to the sparkle; it reduces the *surface tension* and speeds the release of the dissolved gas, resulting in a flat wine in a very short time. To remove the last traces of domestic bleach, after rinsing, a sulphite solution is invaluable, for it has a neutralising action on the bleach and a slight trace of sulphite remaining in the bottle is far more natural to the wine than the chlorine in the bleach (see page 36).

Stoppers and Corks

Sparkling wine made by the champagne method requires two corking operations, one for the secondary fermentation in the bottle and another for the final sealing after disgorging. The object is the same in both instances - to ensure a gas-tight seal capable of withstanding pressures up to 90 lb. p.s.i.

24

A useful bottle-rinsing machine

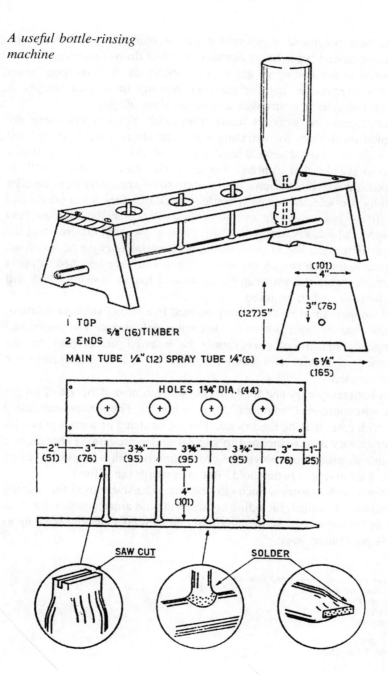

1 TOP
2 ENDS

5/8" (16) TIMBER

MAIN TUBE 1/2" (12) SPRAY TUBE 1/4" (6)

(101)
4"

(127) 5"

3" (76)

6½"
(165)

HOLES 1¾" DIA. (44)

2"
(51)

3"
(76)

3¾"
(95)

3¾"
(95)

3¾"
(95)

3"
(76)

1"
(25)

4"
(101)

SAW CUT

SOLDER

The best polythene stoppers for the second fermentation are the hollow open-end type, because when the yeast drops down finally it is deposited in the hollow of the stopper, thus making disgorging much easier and effective, but for the final bottling the sealed stopper is recommended as it is stronger and reduces the ullage.

Champagne-type stoppers made from clear, taintless polythene are designed specifically for sparkling wines and are reasonably priced and easy to insert. Sound second-hand ones may also be used. Their only disadvantage is that, unlike natural cork, they do not swell to compensate for the various bottle-neck sizes and therefore must be carefully pre-selected for each bottle. Check that they are a good hand tight fit — not over-tight or the sealing rings may be flattened and damaged and a faulty seal will result. Ensure, too, that the crown of the stopper is not too big to prevent the wire muselets (wire hoods) from gripping *below* the rim on the bottle. When you have matched stoppers to bottles, secure them with an elastic band or length of string. They will then be ready when required.

All stoppers must be thoroughly washed in a strong sulphite solution. Do not heat or boil, otherwise distortion will occur. The traditional champagne mushroom cork cannot be inserted successfully by the amateur - a special tool being required — and it is therefore not recommended.

For both temporary and final corking we recommend the use of proper trade wire muselets ("muzzles", or wire hoods). They are not expensive and, with care, may be used twice. The use of string or wire is generally unsatisfactory as it is inclined to slip off under pressure, although it is possible to groove the polythene crown lightly with a length of heated wire, thus giving a better hold. But is it worth the effort?

Crown cork closures. Such closures are extensively used for capping all manner of bottles, including commercial and amateur made beer, as well as for the second fermentation of commercial sparkling wine up to the disgorgement stage.

Supplier for 29mm crowns and applicators:
Vigo Vineyard Supplies
Bollhayes Park
Clayhidon
Cullompton
Devon
EX15 3PN
Tel: 0823 680 230

A Champagne vineyard of the "Cote des Blancs"; the village of Cramant

The yeast settling on the side of the bottle can easily be seen; it will be gradually shaken down on to the cork

Filling a champagne press: the cage of a champagne press is wide but shallow, so that the minimum of colour is imparted to the juice

A remueur at work, twisting the bottles sharply in their "pupitres"

A typical champagne cellar

If there is a disadvantage with crown corks it is the absence of the characteristic "pop" from the bottle on opening, but it is advisable to remove the stopper gently to avoid loss of the precious contents, so why worry?

Crown corks have already been used for the final presentation of the champagne quarter-bottle and it is thought in commercial circles that before very long non-vintage champagne half-bottles will appear on the market capped with them. Once the public has accepted the presentation of half-bottles, no doubt this form of stoppering will be utilised for the standard size non-vintages. It is unlikely that vintage champagne will ever feature anything but the classic natural cork stopper.

Crown corks have the advantages of being less expensive and much more convenient to fit; they also avoid the danger of the rare occasions when the wine may become "corked". Amateurs would be advised to take full advantage of all known modern commercial practices where possible, but until recently these 29 mm. closures were not readily available (beer crowns are 25 mm. and not suitable). We ourselves have had to arrange for the closures to be specially imported from the Société du Bouchon Couronne, France, where the manufacturers have been exceedingly helpful in providing us the design data for the approved applicator tool.

Disgorging is much simplified by using crown corks as is realised by most English professional sparkling winemakers.

The "knock-on" applicator tool works to better advantage when operated by screw pressure. The handiman could easily make use of a wine press or a sash clamp.

Not all champagne bottles will accommodate crown closures and consequently selection has to be made when seeking out the used bottles. All the Moët and Chandon bottles (they appear to be the most common) that we have obtained take crown closures and have the radiused flanges specially designed for the purpose.

Various patent sparkling wine stoppers have been marketed over the years to ease the disgorgement process and one that has stood the test of time has the trade name *Condessa*. This device is currently available and has a sprung loaded valve which relieves excess pressure and may be released to expel the yeast sediment with the bottle inverted. One slight snag, that we found, is that upward excursions of temperature, and hence pressure, caused wine to leak past the valve with the bottle in the horizontal postion. Of course, this may be avoided by keeping it upright,

27

Closures

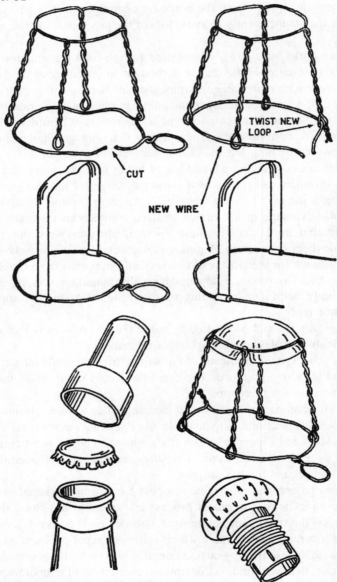

Top: How to re-use wire muselets
Bottom left: crown cork and capping tool
Bottom right: Hollow polythene mushroom stopper

28

but this would deprive the wine of exposure to the track of yeast along the length of the bottle — a significant feature of the *méthod champenoise.*

A good sparkling wine should really be dispensed from a champagne bottle and not from a beer bottle. Just as much prestige is lost from serving sparkling wine in this way as is lost by dispensing still wine from a mineral water or orange squash bottle! Any good wine should be served with ceremony which it rightly deserves. However, newcomers may be excused in their early ventures, especially if disgorging is not envisaged, for screwed stoppered bottles do not lend themselves to it.

Essential Equipment

Second-hand sound champagne bottles
1 litre size bottle crates
Champagne-type polythene stoppers
Clinitest kit
Wire muselets
Simple rack and container for freezing

Authors' note: The Condessa stopper, as fitted to a champagne bottle, is a useful alternative to the 1 pint size screw-capped beer bottle for checking progress of the second fermentation as described on page 80. Then, the valve may be released gently to verify a pressure build-up from further fermentation.

CHAPTER 5

Ingredients to Use

The obvious feature of sparkling wines, of course, is the sparkle, but let us not forget that the basic wine is all-important. It *must* be a wine of the light, fragrant character suitable for the production of sparkling wines — a sparkle is not attractive in a full bodied, heavy-flavoured wine — and this means that our choice of ingredient is crucial.

So, if we are starting out from scratch to produce a sparkling wine, the first decision that we have to make is what the main ingredient of our basic wine is to be.

Generally speaking, it will be found that fruit of one sort or another is the best material, and gives one a better chance of obtaining a well-balanced must. Any imbalance in the must seems to show up even more plainly in a light, delicate sparkling wine than in a still one, and so do imperfections in technique.

Vegetables and grain, in our opinion, are unlikely to provide the quality we seek in a sparkling wine.

Quality of ingredients is certainly the key to successful sparkling wine making, to ensure good balance and flavour, and to assist in bouquet formation. We advocate the use of sound fully-ripe fruit, recently harvested if possible. It takes exactly the same time to produce good wine as it does to make "jungle juice," so we might just as well give our wine every chance by only using the best fruit. The winemaker who has ready access to home-grown or wild fruit is indeed fortunate, since he can pick it at its peak for ripeness by personal assessment of flavour and acidity. Winemakers who are less fortunate, and have to purchase the ingredients, would sometimes be wise to let the fruit ripen at home before proceeding to make the wine. Remember, patience is the first and most important quality of a good winemaker!

The grape. In considering the best possible choice for a sparkling wine, one could certainly do no better than the wine grape, the choice of commercial winemakers all over the world. Unfortunately, these are not generally available to the home winemaker, who normally has to make do with the imported, dessert type of grape, which is characterised by its fleshy nature and is considerably lower in both juice and acid, but this latter deficiency may be easily corrected and its balance made good.

In recent years many enthusiasts have planted vineyards in the southern part of this country, some of considerable acreage. Others, with less space available, have also planted a few vines in their gardens. Most of them have taken advantage of the recommended selection of varieties known to do well in our climate, resulting from the researches of R. Barrington-Brock of the Viticultural Research Station at Oxted in Surrey and incidentally, some good sparkling wine was made there, from the S.V. 5-276 grape. In her writings on the grape vine, Gillian Pearkes has also demonstrated that vine growing is well worthwhile, whether it be on a large or small scale, so we can if we wish make sparkling wine from our own home-grown grapes—a double achievement.

As an alternative, white grape juice concentrate, imported from the continent, is readily available. It is not really expensive and is the next best thing, but be wary of the cheaper grades which tend to be rather dark in colour and thus produce wine of unattractive appearance. In recent years amateur winemakers seem to have drifted away from grape juice concentrates in favour of currently available supermarket 1 litre packs of grape juice. The muscatel variety from Tesco is a favoured choice.

Apple. Many winemakers make a light table-wine of excellent quality, from apples, so why not a sparkling apple? The higher quality apple wines are invariably the result of a blend of cooking and dessert apples and a small supplement of crab apples is useful to provide the requisite degree of astringency, but the quantity used must be limited to avoid harshness. The use of sulphite is essential to avoid the *browning effect* upon the wine of *oxidation* and *enzyme* action. Unripe windfalls, in our opinion, would not be expected to make a quality wine.

Pear. The most suitable types of pear for sparkling wine are to be found in the cooking and perry varieties. Wines made from dessert pears usually produce rather nondescript flavours and are better blended with other fruit bases of stronger character. *Browning* can also be a problem with pears. Sleepy pears should be avoided; the best ones for winemaking are in the condition termed firm-ripe.

Rhubarb is another traditional sparkling wine ingredient; in fact, one of the varieties is known by the name Champagne. We would, however, only consider base wine made from the young tender stalks. The forced varieties in May are the most suitable. The hard woody stuff, rejected for culinary purposes, should be avoided like the plague. Any ingredient not suitable for cooking by virtue of its condition is most certainly wrong for sparkling or any other wine.

Gooseberry. The gooseberry, sometimes called "the hairy grape," provides a flavour reminiscent of the muscatel grape and is an excellent base for a white sparkling wine. Although the hard green gooseberry, harvested in late May and early June, is frequently recommended, we prefer to gather or purchase the fruit in early July, when the berries are softer in texture and considerably richer in juice.

The dessert varieties which become available later in the year do not make such a delicate sparkling wine; both flavour and bouquet tend to be a little overpowering.

The red varieties which ripen and develop colour in August make what can only be described as a delightful rosé sparkling wine, of an appropriately slightly more robust nature.

Gooseberry juice and the extract from the young tender stalks and leaves of grape vine prunings frequently marry to advantage and produce a sparkling wine approaching an authentic character.

Elderflower. There is a love-hate relationship towards elderflower wine. To those dedicated to the cause, and there are many, we would respectfully suggest moderation in the quantity of flowers employed, so as to provide a desirable degree of delicacy. Rather than producing a straight wine, we would prefer to consider elderflower as a bouquet-booster for other bases which are deficient in a natural bouquet.

Apricot. This fruit is another well tried and proven favourite with winemakers, used either as fresh fruit or dried. The clean flavour, good colour and easy handling properties commend it as a base for sparkling, table and dessert wine alike.

As one of our choices for making a sparkling wine we recommend blending apricot with other fruit to give a more subtle vinous flavour than if used on its own. Fresh grape juice is our first choice, with a white grape concentrate (not Muscatel) a good second; apple and pears are good, but are not in season at the same time as fresh apricots so have to be blended as finished wines or used with dried apricots. Try a blend of White Cherry and Apricot for a wine with a difference.

Peach. This is a first class fruit for all wine, but the price for top quality fruit can be high. English peaches stand supreme flavour-wise due to the fact that they are ripe when picked, against continental peaches which are harvested unripe to allow for package and journey time. However, beggars can't be choosers and providing ripe sound peaches are used, a good sparkling wine can be made. We find that by purchasing a few boxes wholesale at market early in August and then dividing them between one or two winemakers, a considerable saving can be made. Cheap over-ripe or damaged fruit is dearest in the long run, so don't be tempted to buy these, as off flavours imparted into wines cannot be removed. As the flavour of peach is not as strong as apricot, blending as previously recommended, need not be resorted to, but it is always possible to blend with grape to advantage if so desired. The bouquet of peach wine can sometimes be suspect, to say the least, and to avoid this common fault we do not recommend pulp fermentation. The acid content is lower than apricot, so check and adjust accordingly.

Strawberry. The very mention of this delicious fruit conjures up pleasant thoughts of summer teas in the garden with fresh luscious strawberries topped up with clotted cream and a sprinkling of caster sugar.

Imagine, then, capturing the delicate flavour and aromatic bouquet of this fruit in a sparkling wine! Summer memories with the "pop of a cork"!

Romancing aside, strawberry is without doubt one of the premier fruits for our purpose: its subtle flavour and light fruity bouquet, plus good sugar content and ease of handling, commend it. Strawberries are reasonably cheap, too, if the purchase is made at the right time, and cheaper still if home grown. Like most fruit, it has some shortcomings—shy in acid and it is of a rather uninviting colour. Both of these minor faults can easily be rectified, a simple titration test for acid adjustment and to bring the colour to a pleasant light rosé, small additions of either dried bilberries, red grape concentrate, or even a few dark red rose petals, will do the trick.

In our opinion, this wine is better medium sweet than dry, but the choice is yours. Blends are always a possibility, but ingredients chosen should complement the light character of this wine and not add a conflicting flavour.

Mead. How about a sparkling Mead? This surely must excite the imagination. Here one combines the gay effervescent sparkle with the reputed aphrodisiacal qualities of honey.....''Sex in a bottle,'' with a vengeance! Barbara Cartland could hardly fail to agree.

How, then, do we make this ''elixir of life''? Remembering as always that our aim is to produce a light, delicately poised, wine of exquisite bouquet. The choice of honey is all important. It must be mildly flavoured, of subtle bouquet, and light in colour (a dark amber colour would be out of character and offend the eye in this type of wine, and would reduce the pleasing, lively effect of the running bead). The honeys recommended are best quality English lime, orange and mild clover. Avoid like the plague any strong heavy flavoured honey such as Mexican Yucatan, Heather and Australian blended honey, this latter may contain Eucalyptus. The golden rule is always to taste and make a careful assessment of flavour. A discriminating palate will quickly discern the delicate from the strong. Unlike fruit, honey lacks the necessary acid and nutrients to ensure a sound fermentation and the quantities given in recipes must be used. As the flavour of honey cannot be controlled, it follows that a repeat of the same recipe will result in slight variations in flavour.

An endless variety of blends can be made with honey as the basic ingredient; the best co-partners in the authors' experience for sparkling mead, are fresh white grape juice, white grape concentrate, apple and pear. The experienced winemaker will no doubt extend these blends and experiment with many more, but the novice is advised to hasten slowly.

It is essential not to exceed the initial starting gravities given in the recipes otherwise it may prove difficult or impossible to start the secondary fermentation. Quantities of honey stated in the recipes can only be approximate, as each batch of honey diluted in the same volume of water will vary slightly and adjustments must be made to arrive at the pre-determined gravity, but suggested quantities are featured in Chapter 7 on recipes.

CHAPTER 6

The Basic Wine

The choice of basic ingredients, and the making of the basic wine, have a direct bearing on the quality of the finished sparkling wine. There is no known magic that can correct gross basic imperfections in the production of sparkling wines because once the wine is in the bottle for the second fermentation, no further corrections are possible (although minor adjustments for balance may be made prior to the second fermentation).

The ingredients which we suggested in the last chapter as being eminently suitable for producing sparkling wine, offer a good variety of flavours and colours of the widest possible appeal, yet still retain the degree of delicacy desired in a sparkling wine. Wine made from a blend of ingredients is often rewarding in that it frequently yields a much better balanced composition as compared with the single-ingredient formulation. Blending of finished wines, in our experince, has rarely proved necessary; but we would certainly be in favour of this procedure as a means of achieving a good balance. It is important, however, to avoid confliction of flavours: elderberry and apricot blended together would be hardly likely to provide the harmony acceptable to sparkling wine. The blending of ingredients is by no means a haphazard mixing of flavours and is something of a test of the winemaker's skill and knowledge.

We start by making a table wine tailored to meet specific requirements. It must be brilliantly clear and not too full in body. White wines should range from neutral to pale straw (a slight green tinge is quite in character). Rosé and red wines are most attractive when the colour is bright and not too dark; tawny reds are out.

The wine should be dry, or nearly so, and the specific gravity must not exceed 1.000.

There should be a definite impression of acidity on the palate to provide the freshness required, but the tannin content should be barely perceptible. The alcohol content should range between 10% and 11% by volume and the wine should be free of any off-flavours.

For white sparkling wines like those of commerce the flavour should be near neutral and vinous in quality, although some winemakers will also like to discover as well a subtle fruitiness. Rosé and red sparkling wines will, of course, require a short pulp fermentation to bring out the requisite intensity of colour.

We ourselves normally prepare our base wine specially for the purpose, since ordinary table wines that we produce are invariably a little too high in alcohol for direct conversion. On the other hand, if you have existing stocks of table wine which are suitable for sparkling wine production by all means use those. Later we tell you how.

Preparation of the Fruit

Use only fully ripe and sound fruit. Amongst it one often finds the odd specimen which may be damaged or exhibiting mildew; this should be discarded. With large fruits, such as apple and pears, one must *first* cut away the affected parts.

Wash the fruit thoroughly to remove dirt and any surface spray materials. Practically all commercially grown produce will have been sprayed with fungicides and other preparations and their effect is somewhat of an unknown quantity.

Equipment and hands must be thoroughly clean, and it is a wise plan to sterilise containers with a metabisulphite solution. A convenient one, containing 1% of sulphur dioxide, may be prepared by dissolving 2½ oz. (74 gm.) of sodium metabisulphite in 1 gallon of cold water. Having used it, just drain the apparatus and do not rinse it with water, for some water supplies may contain spoilage yeasts and bacteria. Any remaining sulphite will be negligible.

Where subsequent pulp fermentation is envisaged remove the stalks of the fruit to avoid upsetting the tannin balance, but where gooseberries are employed, without pulp fermentation, there is really no need to "top and tail" the fruit.

36

Juice Extraction. White sparkling wine bases do *not* benefit from pulp fermentation, for there is a real danger of inducing an unwelcome degree of harshness, not in keeping with the character hoped to be found in a sparkling wine. When processing hard fruits destined for white wine, first break or crush the fruit to facilitate effective extraction of the juice. Either use a mincer, in sound condition and preferably fitted with stainless steel cutters, or employ an electric juicer which automatically ejects the pulp. Some fruit extremely rich in natural acid, such as the green gooseberry, may pick up iron contamination from ordinary steel cuttters, to give rise to haze problems. However, the contact time is so short that we feel that no serious hazard is likely to occur. When contact with iron or steel is unavoidable it would, however, be a wise precaution to include some citric acid in the formulation, as this acid will counteract iron hazes by forming a soluble complex. When using an electric juicer it is sometimes desirable to combine the extracted juice with the rejected pulp, to ensure a greater yield on extraction of the juice content.

If only pure juice is used, some winemakers utilise the spent skins (or pulp) to make what is called a "second wash" by fermenting on these skins to produce a "plonk" wine.

We hesitate to recommend the use of liquidisers, as the high maceration rate may release excess tannin and bitterness from the skins.

Now add *cold* water to the fruit pulp, the exact quantity depending upon the juice content of the fruit conerned. Some fruits are naturally juicy and others contain a greater proportion of solid matter. Most berries generally yield more juice than do hard fruits, such as apples.

Little gain in extraction is realised by employing hot or boiling water, and heat, apart from releasing unwanted pectin, can drive off some of the volatile fruit esters which assist in providing the wine with a bouquet. Bouquet is an elusive element in most amateur-made wines, so our techniques are directed towards conserving and encouraging it.

Rohament P is an *enzyme* preparation which will break down the cellular tissue of fruit pulp, and in so doing increases the effectiveness of juice extraction. Pulp is the operative word — it is not fully effective unless the fruit is finely divided. It performs this function without loss of vitamins, colour and flavour—according to the trade literature.

The amateur of today is indeed fortunate in having access to a number of *enzymes* and other additives for winemaking. An *enzyme* is of a complex nature — at least to most of us. They sometimes occur naturally, in yeast for instance; but others are specially prepared for diverse application in industry. Use is made of their function to bring about and/or accelerate particular changes which otherwise would be unacceptably slow. Such is the case for Rohament P. This particular *enzyme* is not an alternative for the *pectolytic enzymes,* under various trade names mentioned later in the chapter; and where used in conjunction with one of these, we would be hesitant in recommending the unconditional use for the preparation of a sparkling wine. An excess of *enzymes* remaining in the wine is thought to have an adverse effect upon the quality and to be certain of avoiding this it is necessary to *pasteurise* the *must* by raising its temperature to the range 66°C-71°C (150°F-160°F) for a short time.

Unfortunately, this heating effect upon the *must* would tend to drive off volatile substances which contribute towards the make-up of the bouquet. These, we are endeavouring to retain. However, where just a *pectolytic enzyme* is used on its own, it is not absolutely necessary to *pasteurise*—in fact, we do not know of any winemakers who actually do this.

The Use of Sulphite. In order to minimise bacterial infections and suppress wild yeasts, both of which may give off flavours, it is essential to add sulphite to the must. Sulphite is the usual name given by winemakers to the active ingredient, sulphur dioxide gas.

A convenient way to introduce sulphite is to add a carefully controlled quantity of a 10% solution of sodium metabisulphite. This solution is easily made up by dissolving 2 oz. of the compound in 20 oz. (1 pint) of cold previously boiled water. This will usually retain its effective strength for about three months. Some readers may prefer to use potassium metabisulphite in place of the sodium salt. For health reasons we should avoid the intake of sodium as far as possible. But, for sterilising equipment use sodium metabisulphite - it is considerably cheaper and more readily obtainable.

The amount of sulphite contained in a *must* or wine is normally expressed in so many parts per million (p.p.m.) but some more advanced texts prefer to use mg. per litre as the measure. The figures quoted are the same in both instances, so no confusion should arise. In the sparkling wine base the working level should be 100 p.p.m. and this concentration requires 10 ml. of 10% solution per gallon. This is best dispensed from a measuring cylinder, but as an alternative the solution may be measured out from a standard 5 ml. medicinal teaspoon. The volumes of domestic teaspoons vary enormously and considerable error may be introduced unless these teaspoons are checked for capacity.

Some winemakers add their sulphite in the form of Campden tablets, and two such tablets per gallon would conveniently provide 100 p.p.m. of sulphite. We, like many other winemakers, prefer to avoid the use of these tablets in winemaking, however, as they are known to contain binding agents to facilitate shaping during manufacture and to retain firm conditions for handling. These binding agents may, under certain circumstances, induce hazes in the wine which are difficult to eradicate.

Sulphite suppresses undesirable bacteria and spoilage yeasts; it also preserves the colour and minimises *oxidation*. An *oxidised* flavour in a sparkling wine is something to avoid at all costs. Sulphite will also tend to increase the glycerine produced as a side effect of the fermentation, providing that smoothness which is essential in a well-balanced wine. When a must has been sulphited it is essential to delay 24 hours before introducing the active yeast starter. By this time the sulphite activity will have been reduced to a safe level, when it no longer retards the action of a wine yeast. In fact, much of the sulphite becomes fixed in combination with other trace compounds of the must, that which takes an active part is known as the free sulphite. The level of acid present in the must bears a direct relationship to the sulphite activity, as the acid will release free sulphur dioxide gas from the added sodium metabisulphite.

Pectin removal. Pectin is a gelatinous compound found in most fruits and some vegetables in varying proportions and can hamper juice extraction. Jellification caused by heating fruit pulp may be part of the jam-making process, but an excess in wine *musts* is decidedly unwelcome. The presence of pectin in our wines may stabilise other hazes and produce a permanent cloudiness, which usually will not respond to a fining agent. Fruit normally contains natural enzymes and providing the must has not been over-heated, these indigenous enzymes will break down the pectin present during the fermentation, so that submicroscopic particles of fruit pulp held in suspension will eventually gravitate out at the end of the fermentation to provide a clear wine.
In some cases the natural enzymes cannot cope with an abnormally high pectin concentration. This is especially the case with early gooseberries, and even when the *cold water method* has been employed pectin will sometimes come through to the finished wine unless the enzyme content is augmented artificially.

Commercially marketed *pectolytic enzymes* are available as found under various trade names and these should be added to musts where an excess of pectin is known to be present, but should not be added to all musts as a matter of course, especially where there is reason to believe that the pectin content is particularly low. Should a haze of pectin origin be encountered at a later stage in the processing, correction could be applied at the time with the use of an adequate quantity of a *pectolytic enzyme.*

A simple test as to whether a haze is caused by pectin is to add four volumes of methylated spirit to one volume of the must or wine; if gelatinous clots form, undue pectin is present.

In using these enzyme preparations manufacturers recommended quantities should be followed, for a large excess of enzyme remaining in the must is not conducive to quality. In suspension the enzymes are most active in the temperature region of 50°C. (122°F.) and are unaffected by normal concentrations of sulphite. However, we would not raise the temperature of the must that high for reasons already given; we prefer a slower activity over a longer period of time.

These enzyme preparations are adversely affected by unusually high temperatures before use, so must be stored under cool conditions; a refrigerator is ideal for the purpose. And they have a limited shelf-life, so should only be purchased from reputable suppliers, who have a rapid turn-over in stock.

The Infusion Process. Having added the desired quantity of cold water to the treated pulp, which should be under the protection of our guardian, sulphite, and have received the *minimum* of enzyme preparations, two days should be allowed for the useful products and flavours to be leached out from the pulp. An occasional stir will help. A plastic container with a well-fitting lid is convenient at this stage. Pulp fermentation for the rosé and red wines is discussed where applicable under the heading of Recipes.

Pulp separation. To separate the diluted juice extract from the pulp, the infusion is either strained through a nylon mesh bag or is processed, with greater ease, by means of a wine press, should this be available. The cage of the press should be lined with a strong fabric bag and we have found tailor's canvas to be eminently suitable for this purpose. It is most important to boil this canvas in several changes of water to remove the dressing. Should this dressing be permittted to remain in the fabric the transfer of contained starch could very well promote a stubborn haze in the wine. As an alternative, a double thickness of nylon

40

mesh, in bag form, might be more convenient to employ as a pulp retainer.

Over-pressing must be avoided at all costs; the action should be one of squeezing rather than of pressing. There is no advantage to be gained by forcing out the last drop of moisture from the pulp, as excessive pressure may well release undesirable substances which could generate an unacceptable degree of harshness as well as providing a haze problem. The free-run, which comes away initially from the press, always provides the potentially best quality wine, and this will normally fall bright and clear so that no fining is necessary.

The Settling Process. The run-out from the press or straining bag should be transferred to a clear glass container, where it should be allowed to rest for one day. During this time the minute particles of fruit pulp debris, small enough to have passed through the mesh of the straining bag, will settle out as a sediment. This process is standard practice on the Continent where quality wines are made, and in France is called *débourbage*. Should the debris be permitted to carry through to the fermentation, unrewarding off-flavours may be developed and could mar the delicate flavour of the wine. Some winemakers filter or fine the *must* at this stage, but we feel that *débourbage* is quite adequate to provide the clear *must* we seek in preparing the basis for our sparkling wines. Obviously, when limited pulp fermentation is carried out for rosé and red sparkling wines, this procedure is not possible: but with the strength of flavour associated with these wines it is unlikely that the omission would detract from the character expected.

Sugar Addition. The cleansed must is now ready to receive the additional sugar to generate approximately 10% of alcohol during fermentation into wine; but before adding any sugar we feel it would be a good idea to consider the common types of sugar available for this purpose.

Glucose has been advocated by some winemakers, who feel that it is more natural to wine than is cane sugar, sucrose. In fact, they claim that cane sugar can give rise to a degree of harshness in the resultant wine. We cannot go along with this assertion as our own experience has failed to support any such findings, especially as we *know* that cane sugar is employed to sweeten champagne following *dégorgement*. Glucose is, incidentally, considerably more expensive than cane sugar. It is manufactured from starch-containing products, and if used, it is important to be of B.P. or food quality grades. This would avoid the danger of introducing free starch into the wine, with consequent risk of haze formation. To check for the presence of starch is easy enough: one merely adds one or two drops of tincture of iodine to a separate solution of the glucose; the presence of starch is indicated by an intense blue coloration.

Invert Sugar. This is widely used in the brewing industry, where quick fermentations are the order of the day. As far as fermentation is concerned, both glucose and invert sugar give the yeast a flying start. The enzymes associated with the yeast do not have to fulfil a conversion process to *hydrolyse* the sugar, as is necessary with cane sugar, before the fermentation gets under way. But this is not really important as the net result is the same for cane, glucose, and invert sugars in that a given hydrometer reading for any of the sugars would be expected to provide an identical alcohol content in the finished wine, other conditions being equal.

Your authors plump for the good old white granulated stuff in 1 kgm. packets and are quite happy with the results. Why use anything else? The specific gravity of the sugar-adjusted must is chosen to lie between 1.065 and 1.075 as measured at 15.5°C. (60°F.) Temperatures departing significantly from this value will critically alter the true sugar assessment; and where departures are concerned, the reader is advised to consult this table.

TABLE 1

TEMPERATURE CORRECTION TABLE

Temperature		Specific Gravity	Gravity
°C.	°F.	Correction	Correction
10	50	—0.001	—1
15	**59**	**none**	**none**
20	68	+0.001	+1
25	77	+0.002	+2
30	86	+0.003	+3
35	95	+0.005	+5
40	104	+0.007	+7

42

Example (see page 75)
Wine temperature 25°C. (77°F.)

S.G. required	1.000	0
Correction	0.002	2
Adjust sugar to	0.998	—2

Winemakers must appreciate that exact sugar additions cannot be specified, as the amount of sugar extracted from a given quantity of fruit pulp will vary considerably, depending upon the type of fruit used and its degree of ripeness. The hydrometer, in conjunction with illustrated sugar tables, must be employed to arrive at our recommended sugar content. It must be pointed out that sugar tables have been worked out empirically on the basis of a wine grape juice. Such juices generally contain a greater proportion of unfermentable substances than do our own diluted extracts. The inflation in specific gravity due to these substances does not contribute to the alcohol content. To make allowance for this consideration we have deliberately chosen a specific gravity range in an attempt to avoid developing too much alcohol in the wine. It is important not to over-tax the yeast in the bottle fermentation stage, where the factors which influence fermentation are far more critical than experienced in making the base wine at atmospheric pressure. These factors will be discussed more fully in Chapter 10.

Acidity correction. As we mentioned earlier, for a basic wine which is to be "sparkled", there should be a distinct impression of acidity on the palate and this should come through over the taste of the sugar. We normally check our acidity by the *titration method* and include details of this in Appendix A. The value is expressed in terms of sulphuric acid, for convenience, and should be something like 4 to 5 parts per thousand. Winemakers generally delay becoming involved with measuring procedure until they have gained some measure of experience in winemaking. Having once gained this experience they would, of course, have developed discriminating palates, we hope, so that the need for scientific measurement becomes less important. When in doubt on tasting, it is always a good idea to seek a second opinion from a colleague or another member of the household. Whatever chemical analysis shows, it is the flavour of the acid on the palate which is the true assessment as far as acid balance is concerned. There should be

43

TABLE 2
GRAVITY TABLE

Specific Gravity	Grav.	British lb./gal.	U.S.A. lb./gal.	gm./l.	Potential alcohol % by vol.	Balling or Brix	Twadell Baume	
1.005	5	0.0	0.0	0	0.0	1.8	1.0	0.7
1.010	10	0.13	0.10	13	0.8	3.0	2.0	1.4
1.015	15	0.27	0.23	27	1.6	4.1	3.0	2.2
1.020	20	0.40	0.33	40	2.3	5.3	4.0	2.8
1.025	25	0.53	0.44	53	3.1	6.5	5.0	3.5
1.030	30	0.66	0.55	66	3.9	7.7	6.0	4.2
1.035	35	0.79	0.66	79	4.7	8.8	7.0	4.9
1.040	40	0.93	0.78	93	5.4	9.9	8.0	5.6
1.045	45	1.06	0.88	106	6.2	11.1	9.0	6.2
1.050	50	1.19	0.99	119	7.0	12.3	10.0	6.9
1.055	55	1.32	1.10	132	7.8	13.4	11.0	7.5
1.060	60	1.46	1.22	146	8.6	14.5	12.0	8.2
1.065	65	1.59	1.33	159	9.3	15.7	13.0	8.8
1.070	**70**	**1.72**	**1.43**	**172**	**10.1**	**16.9**	**14.0**	**9.4**
1.075	75	1.86	1.55	186	10.8	18.0	15.0	10.1
1.080	80	1.99	1.66	199	11.7	19.2	16.0	10.7
1.085	85	2.12	1.77	212	12.4	20.4	17.0	11.3
1.090	90	2.26	1.90	226	13.2	21.5	18.0	11.9
1.095	95	2.39	1.99	239	14.0	22.6	19.0	12.5
1.100	100	2.52	2.10	252	14.8	23.7	20.0	13.1

sufficient acid present at the beginning to ensure a sound fermentation and to reduce the possibilities of bacterial infections which could cause all manner of nasty off flavours in the wine. The originators of many old-fashioned recipes (which are constantly repeated) did not take acidity at all seriously and frequently herbs had to be added to hide the unpleasant flavours of the bacterial infections which were invariably due to the lack of acid. The herbs used to flavour commercial vermouths are today considered integral with the character, but originally they disguised an inadequacy in the wine.

When composing a basic wine, without the use of titration, the acidity is best adjusted, by taste, before the addition of sugar. Its presence would obscure the sensation on the palate. But, if a titration is employed the sugar should be present and, following the initial titration the requisite quantity of acid may be determined, added and checked. Latterly, we have favoured working nearer to 4 p.p.t and even below.

Where we require to increase the acidity, equal quantities of malic and tartaric acids are to be preferred, because these acids are natural to wine, whereas citric acid is not; and furthermore, citric acid is far more susceptible to bacterial infections, so is best avoided as the *sole* acid in sparkling wines. Should the acidity require reduction one can, of course, dilute with additional water (providing the character of body and flavour will withstand the dilution), but this requires the correction of the sugar content. An alternative is to accept the existing degree of acidity and later blend with another wine containing less acid.

Carbonates of sodium and potassium are frequently suggested to reduce the acidity, but both these compounds may induce peculiar flavours when used in excess, *especially after fermentation.* Where tartaric acid is present, neutral potassium tartrate is useful. And, expressed as sulphuric acid, 1 p.p.t. (1 gm./litre) is neutralised by 2.3 gm./litre of this compound; but no more than 3 p.p.t. should be treated this way to avoid off-flavours. For one Brit. gallon, .35 oz. will be required for each p.p.t. of acidity.

pH Measurement. Many winemakers have been misled, in our opinion, by being encouraged to measure their acidities solely with narrow range pH papers. Admittedly, the method is simple to perform and does provide a good indication of acid *activity,* but it does not necessarily relate directly to the true impression of acidity gained by the palate. However, pH measurement in conjunction with titration data does provide the wine chemist with useful information, but is of little real value to the amateur practitioner. Our recommended acidity level of 4 p.p.t. as sulphuric is considered to provide a sufficiently low pH value to combat bacterial infection.

The titration method provides a more realistic guide in assessing the degree of acidity in the *must* or wine. Malic acid is more active on the palate than is tartaric acid. The former is said to promote an apple-flavoured acidity, so should not be permitted to dominate in a sparkling wine. Commercially, a malo-lactic fermentation is frequently encouraged to reduce this acid, when the wine is too sharp.

Finally, we would advise our readers to carry out their titrations before adding the nutrient salts. These salts contain phosphates which

45

act as what the chemists refer to as 'buffering agents'. The presence of an excess of a buffering agent invariably causes a poor end point to the titration, in that the colour change is not clear and may be extended over several drops from the burette. This can lead to inaccuracies and be most confusing to the "amateur analyst."

Nutrients. When it is necessary to dilute the fruit juices with water to reduce the acidity and strength of flavour, as is quite often the case, the concentration of naturally occurring mineral salts and vitamins present will suffer a sympathetic reduction. It is essential to make good this depletion in nutrient content. The presence of adequate nutrition at the beginning of the fermentation is vital to build up a strong colony of yeast cells and to ensure that these cells prosper and multiply to replace the ones that die off during the ensuing fermentation. The principal requirement is that of nitrogen and this is conveniently made available in a form which is easily assimilated by the yeast, with the addition of diammonium phosphate. The phosphate radical also enters into the complex series of reactions which take place during fermentation; so this di-ammonium phosphate fulfills a two-fold purpose. It is essential to use B.P. or food quality chemicals in winemaking as the impurities sometimes found in commercial grades can have an adverse effect upon the subsequent fermentation.

Generally the ammonium compound on its own proves to be adequate, but this could be supplemented to advantage with potassium phosphate and magnesium sulphate. The presence of ammonium phosphate is said to limit the quantity of fusel oil produced during the fermentation as a side reaction. Fusel oil is a mixture of higher alcohols, mainly isomeric amyl alcohol and an excess present in the wine detracts from the quality we seek.

Some winemakers use proprietary nutrient tablets, which are reputed to contain all the necessary mineral and vitamin requirements. They are somewhat expensive, but certainly convenient to use. The following formulation, suggested by Bryan Acton, may be used to good purpose and compounds are usually obtainable from a pharmacist or winemakers' suppliers:

Di-ammonium hydrogen phosphate—1 gm. per litre or 1 teaspoon per gallon.

Potassium phosphate—½ gm. per litre or ½ teaspoon per gallon.

Magnesium sulphate—¼ teaspoon per gallon.

Malt extract and Marmite have been proposed as nutrients, but we feel

46

that the flavour of these preparations might be detected in a delicate wine, and we would hesitate to recommend their use in the formulation of a sparkling wine.

Tannin is an organic compound, which occurs naturally in the skins and stalks of fruit in varying quantities. Its inclusion in the wine influences the general balance by providing a degree of astringency. Where this is lacking the wine is sometimes said to be flabby, and devoid of zest. In white grape wines the tannin content is relatively low, about 0.4 gm. per litre. Not all red fruits are necessarily rich in tannin but it would be true to say that elderberries and red grapes are generally well endowed. A sparkling wine made from fruit rich in tannin should be fermented on the skins for a short period only, to facilitate the removal of a moderate amount of colour; otherwise the tannin extracted at the same time will render the resultant wine far too astringent to suit the delicacy expected for our purposes. As a rough guide, for fruit shy in tannin, 0.4 gm. per litre (a salt spoonful per gallon) would be in order for a potential sparkling wine. Tannin can, of course, be added after fermentation is complete and at that stage it would be easier to assess the degree of astringency, but as tannin is useful in clearing the wine, advantage is gained by making the addition at the *must* stage. **We deplore the use of cold tea to provide tannin in our formulations— the colour alone would spoil the character of the wine.**

The yeast. In the production of champagne and commercial sparkling wines a true champagne yeast culture is not always used for the initial fermentation process, but *must* always be used for the final fermentation. **We would recommend that the amateur vintner should always use a true champagne culture throughout the entire process.**

We attach great importance to getting the fermentation under way as soon as possible. This philosophy is applied generally to our wine *musts,* as all the time a *must* lies inactive there is a possibility of bacterial infection, especially if insufficient sulphite has been used. Once fermentation has begun, the alcohol formed in conjunction with the sulphite and acid will act as preservatives to minimise the growth of undesirable moulds and bacteria.

When this book was first published the only true and reliable champagne yeast, available to the amateur winemaker, was in the form of an agar slope or a liquid culture; powdered and tableted yeast, at that time, were considered to be of doubtful origin and unreliable. This situation has changed in recent times, mainly due to the research work carried out by Professor Gerry Fowles who ran the Oenology Research Laboratory at Reading University, until his recent retirement, where he tested and procured a wide range of yeasts suitable for all styles of wine. In his private capacity he has made available, under the trade name of Gervin, a range of yeasts especially for the amateur winemaker. These are of a granular nature and hermetically sealed in foil sachets, each sachet containing sufficient yeast for five gallons of wine. The champagne yeast selected and recommended is Varietal C, a Saccharomyces Bayanus strain EC 1118. This yeast, we understand, is used by 70% of commercial vintners—a worthy testimonial to be sure.

To make up a gallon of wine use about half the contents of a sachet which is added to approximately 25 ml of lukewarm water (35-40°C) with a pinch of sugar and after about 15 minutes stir vigorously before adding to the prepared must. Although not absolutely necessary for larger quantities, say 5 gallons, we would prefer to make up a starter to ensure fermentation of the main bulk takes place as quickly as possible. This is made by preparing the yeast as in the case of the one gallon lot, but using the whole sachet and then adding it to a litre of supermarket white grape juice to be contained in a loosely covered bottle. This starter should be prepared 2 to 3 days beforehand to permit sufficient time for the yeast colony to multiply. The grape juice is readily obtainable from your local supermarket.

Supplier for champagne yeast:

Gervin Supplies
61 Church Road
Woodley
Reading
Berks

Tel: 0734-691518

The Fermentation. Yeast activity becomes apparent first of all by a gradual increase in the level of cloudiness. This is called the *lag-phase* and during this time the colony of cells is multiplying. The fermentation will not begin until the colony has increased its population to about 30 million cells per fluid ounce (30 ml.) During this time isolated islands of yeast froth often appear on the surface of the must. These gradually extend in area until the whole surface is covered completely and when this has happened, there is apparent gas evolution from the surface which will increase in intensity as the fermentation becomes fully active. The peak of effervescence may not be realised for two days.

In order to build up a strong yeast colony at the beginning of the fermentation it is essential to have an adequate supply of oxygen present in the must. This is known as the *aerobic* phase. Sufficient oxygen will usually be present in the water used in the preparation, but boiling of the water, which we do not advocate unless sterilisation is required, appreciably reduces the oxygen content. Sulphite added at the beginning of must preparation, for good reason, does in fact absorb some oxygen, but the loss does not significantly reduce the effective level required to support sound yeast growth. Sulphite is what the chemists term a "reducing agent."

When fermentation is active, the dense cloud of carbon dioxide gas covering the must will not permit the entry of any more oxygen from the atmosphere and creates *an aerobic* condition. Once the fermentation is fully active the yeast no longer requires *aerobic* conditions and it will derive its energy from the sugar. At an ambient temperature of 18°C. (65°F.) the fermentation would be expected to be complete in 2-3 weeks. We normally leave a hydrometer in the fermenting must to observe the fall in gravity, which will be extremely rapid in the first few days. Once this primary fermentation is over and the frothing has subsided, the must should be transferred to a bottle and a fermentation lock fitted, however, the layer of carbon dioxide gas above the must will exclude air during the secondary fermentation. At the end of the fermentation the wine (it is no longer a must) will then begin to clear, and the specific gravity should be near .990. The air space (ullage) must be minimised to reduce oxidation.

Importance of Temperature

Wherever people meet, the traditional opening gambit of conversation always seems to be about the weather and prevailing temperature, it's either too wet or too dry, too hot, or perishing cold; we never seem satisfied!

All too few amateur winemakers fully appreciate or understand the important part temperature plays in wine production and they do little to assist or effect control. Taking "pot luck" fermenting wines in airing cupboards, lofts, garages and sheds with wide fluctuating temperature is not conducive to good quality and it is well worth time and effort to improvise some form of insulation and temperature control during fermentation. This is particularly true in the case of sparkling wine, at secondary bottle fermentation stage. We rely solely on the labour of yeast and co-enzymes to perform the miracle of fermentation and it is surely logical to give them the best possible conditions to work in. Sound recipe formulation ensures primary basic needs and the correct temperature gives optimum working conditions. Yeast, being a living organism of the fungi group, is as influenced by temperature change as any other form of organic life and sudden changes of temperature can be as damaging to it as it would to a delicate hot-house plant, but fortunately for us yeast can live in and tolerate a wide range of temperatures, between 5°C. (33°F.) to 32°C. (90°F.), depending upon yeast strain, etc. The best temperature for growth is 21°C. (70°F.) to 28°C. (82°F.) This is the ideal range for preparing cultures and starter bottles, also for getting the initial ferment under way.

Once fermentation is progressing satisfactorily it is recommended that for high quality white wines the temperature is gradually reduced to 15.5°C. (60°F.) for the rest of the fermentation as at this temperature there is a lower loss of volatile esters and aldehydes. It is also necessary to understand that the energy expended by the yeast during fermentation will raise the temperature of the must and unless this can dissipate freely through the walls of the fermentation vessel it may reach as high as 35°C. (95°F.) to 38°C. (100°F.) Should this occur the fermentation will "stick" and apart from the danger of bacterial spoilage it will be difficult to get the wine restarted due to the yeast producing toxic substances (known as mannitic infection).

Generally speaking, these conditions do not arise with small batch production in one- or two-gallon containers, but winemakers using ten gallon carboys would be well advised to check for temperature rises and if necessary remove some of the protecting straw packing of the cage to allow the heat to dissipate. Take care, for the glass is very thin at the waist. Another reason for advocating lower temperature fermentation is that there is far less risk of infection by bacteria and that the preventive dose of SO_2 (sulphur dioxide—sulphite) can be proportionally smaller. The latter is most desirable as the total free SO_2 (sulphur dioxide-sulphite) should be kept to a minimum as not only would a high SO_2 level make secondary fermentation difficult but the pungent smell is more noticeable when the wine is served due to the lively effervescence releasing volatile esters. The size and design of fermentation cupboards, boxes, etc., must be dictated by individual needs and available space.

All electrical heaters and thermostats must be correctly wired and fused. Small wattage heaters sold for placing under car radiators are ideal. Don't use electric light bulbs as a source of heat; exposing wine to any form of light for long periods is detrimental. Room thermostats are robust and reliable and easily fitted and are best placed on the opposite side to the heaters. Always check temperature with a good thermometer. Any insulating material must be fireproof. Double walled design is preferred with the insulating material packed in between. The inside surface can then be painted to give a smooth surface easy to clean and mop up any accidental spillage. Some winemakers claim success with the use of small fish-tank heaters and thermostats. These are sterilised and then suspended in the container; they give some degree of heat control and the local heat given off has not been found to be detrimental to the yeast or must.

As the equipment for raising temperature is relatively simple to install and is reasonably priced compared to any type of refrigerating plant necessary to lower temperature, it follows that the best time to plan your production of sparkling wine is during the autumn or late spring when the temperatures are not too high and minimum artificial heat correction is required.

The temperatures for aftercare and storage of wine are dealt with in Chapter 11.

Fermenting Under Pressure

The effect of pressure. Where large closed vats are used in the modern commercial wineries the rate of fermentation is frequently controlled by working under pressure. The escape of the carbon dioxide gas evolved during the fermentation is governed by means of a pressure relief valve. A fast rate of fermentation, which is undesirable for the production of quality wine, is either caused by the heat generated by the *exothermic* nature of the fermentation or by a high prevailing ambient temperature in the winery. This latter effect is most prevalent in the hotter wine producing countries, such as Spain.

We have had limited but most encouraging experience in this field by fitting pressure relief valves to suitably designed fermentation containers, and the small scale plant which we designed for the *cuve close* or tank method, for the secondary fermentation, has been invaluable. Not only can we regulate the pressure between 10 and 50 p.s.i., but it is also possible to withdraw samples of the fermenting wine to check the specific gravity. This means that we are able to adjust the setting of the valve so that the rate of the primary fermentation may be controlled; and in this way, during particularly hot spells, the bouquet forming substances in the wine are not boiled off during what might be a somewhat violent fermentation.

It is **imperative** that pressure controlled fermentations be conducted in containers which will safely withstand the pressure, and that the valves employed are completely reliable and are not likely to become blocked by fruit pulp thrown up by the fermentation and rendered inoperative. One gallon and other glass bottles would *not* be suitable for this purpose and all other containers should be pressure tested to the satisfaction of the winemaker.

The effect of daylight upon fermentation. The ultra-violet radiation of direct sunlight has an adverse effect upon yeast activity, and so does indirect daylight to a much lesser extent. Therefore, fermenting musts should be protected from direct ultra-violet radiation. Fermenting 1-gallon jars on the window ledge may look very attractive, but a much sounder fermentation would be realised by hiding these bottles away in a dark cupboard or by simply wrapping the bottles with opaque paper.

Containers. Where 1-gallon musts are being considered, it is wise to carry out the early stages of fermentation in covered 2-gallon polythene or polypropylene containers. However, the must can equally well be split up into two 1-gallon bottles to cope with the frothy conditions frequently encountered in early stages of fermentation. Fermentation locks are not necesssary at this stage and polythene film secured with an elastic band would provide an adequate covering.

For larger volume musts winemakers frequently use domestic plastic bins. Prolonged storage in such containers is not to be recommended, but where used we would favour the lightest coloured plastic to minimise the danger of contamination from the mineral fillers present in the material.

Containers of food quality plastic are preferred for quality wine production and are readily available from winemakers' suppliers. For storage of white wines and sparkling wine bases glass containers are the best possible choice. However, in the larger sizes these glass bottles are becoming more difficult to obtain and stocks already purchased must, by virtue of their fragility, be considered as expendable. Glazed earthenware jars are quite suitable and have the advantage of being considerably more robust, but of course do not permit, *in situ,* visual examination of the wine. Wooden casks are not the best choice for white wine storage, especially in the smaller 5 gallon capacities, as *oxidation* can be a problem. Coating the outside of the cask with polyurethane lacquer does offset the degree of *oxidation* and your authors have treated some of their own casks in this way, but hesitate to use these for the prolonged storage of sparkling wine bases.

When the fermentation is complete and no more carbon dioxide gas is freely escaping from the wine, there will be a heavy sediment composed mainly of dead yeast cells and the wine itself will be cloudy. This is due to the suspension of yeast cells which has yet to gravitate out, but this cloudiness may also be caused by other suspended tiny particles, which may fall out in the course of time; however, they may, on the other hand, require physical or chemical assistance in order to render the wine completely brilliant. With these thoughts in mind we follow with a chapter (8) on racking clarification and assessment, but let's have a look at the recipe section beforehand.

CHAPTER 7

Recipes for basic wines

The winemaker may well have a light table wine already in his possession which would be suitable to be provided with a "sparkle" and it would be a good idea to have a look at existing stocks before proceeding to select one of our recipes. This would save considerable time in arriving at one's goal and even if the wine does not conform exactly to our own critical standards it would provide the desirable experience to "get the feel" of the *méthode champenoise* before embarking upon a more ambitious scale of production.

Before proceeding to the second fermentation the reader would be wise to ensure that the wine's sulphite content is on the low side. An excess of sulphite can impede or even inhibit the bottle fermentation and the pungent and unpleasant odour of sulphite will be exaggerated in the bouquet of the wine, due to the effervescence. We have observed this failing in some of the cheaper commercial sparkling wines.

An excess of sulphite is immediately and obviously apparent both by tasting and "nosing" the wine and may be reduced by deliberately introducing oxygen from the air.

The oxygen will combine with the sulphite to reduce its level and the very small amount of sulphuric acid so formed will have no effect upon the quality of the wine. The method we recommend is to "pitch" the wine from one container to another with violent splashing and the oxygen so introduced will also assist in good yeast growth for the fermentation in the bottle.

Obviously, no proprietary wine stabiliser or potassium sorbate must be present for such additives are irreversible, and the wine must be dry. Most amateur-made table wines are generally stronger in flavour and alcohol than their commercial counterparts and will stand some degree of dilution to reduce the strength of flavour and alcohol level to our recommended starting points for the secondary fermentation. If the history of the wine be known, records will indicate how much alcohol is present, and then the additional water needed to provide the requisite alcoholic strength may be derived from the following formula:

$$\text{(vol of water)} = \text{(orig. vol)} \times \frac{\text{(orig. alc \%)}}{\text{(req alc \%)}} - \text{(orig. vol)}$$

Example 4.51 (1 gall) 13% alcohol adjusted to 11%

$$4.5 \times \frac{13}{11} - 4.5 = .8201 \text{ (820 ml.) (29 fl. oz.)}$$

Remember, flavour and colour light, alcohol 10-11% specific gravity 1.000 or below.

It is a wise precaution to try a small-scale pilot experiment in, say, a 1-pint screw-capped beer or cider bottle, just to make sure that the wine chosen will actually respond to a second fermentation before proceeding to follow the text in the appropriate chapters which describe the detailed procedures for processing the wine.

Recipes

The following recipes have been formulated to produce a suitable base-wine, well balanced and delicate in flavour, with a pre-determined amount of alcohol which will ensure sound keeping qualities, but not inhibit yeast activity during the secondary fermentation in the bottle or tank.

The recipes using Grape and Gooseberry produce wines resembling the character of traditional champagne, whilst the other recipes will appeal to winemakers who prefer a distinct but not overpowering flavour of the particular fruit used. All these selected recipes have been well tried, are familiar to the authors, and have in our opinion proved to be most successful.

Recipes for making one gallon have been specified, but larger quantities can obviously be made by scaling up the ingredients in proportion to the volume required, with one exception — the yeast culture, which is more than adequate to ferment up to 5-10 gallons from a single starter preparation.

Some winemakers may question the necessity of the one-day settling out period for the must; but experience has proved beyond doubt that it is well worth the time taken. By starting with a relatively clear must free from extraneous matter a cleaner flavour is produced and any necessary fining or filtering is made much easier.

Notes on the Recipes

Sulphite. A 10% solution is prepared by dissolving 2 oz. (50 gm.) of sodium metabisulphite in cold water and by making up to 20 fl. oz. (500 ml.). 10 ml. of this solution is equivalent to 2×5 ml. medicinal teaspoons or 2 Campden tablets.

Nutrient salts. Di-ammonium phosphate, which usually proves adequate on its own, may be replaced by proprietary nutrient tablets or by the formulation on page 46.

Tannin. Either grape tannin or B.P. quality tannin may be used. 1/15th oz. (2 gm.) is roughly equivalent to a mustard-spoonful of the compound. It is difficult to specify exact commonplace measures for small quantities.

Pectolytic enzymes. Pectinol and Pektolase should be used according to suppliers' instructions and the quantities *must* not be in excess of those specified.

Water. We assume that a sterile mains water supply will be used, but where other sources are employed it must be clean, fresh and free from infection. The boiling of water drives off the oxygen, which would promote sound yeast growth, and should this be thought necessary aeration will be required.

Yeast starters. See page 47.

Pulp fermentation, in our opinion, is not recommended for the white sparkling wines, but limited fermentation on the pulp will naturally be required to extract the requisite degree of colour of the rosé and light red types of sparkling wine.

All added chemical compounds must be of B.P. or food quality and it is most inadvisable to employ commercial grades, for instance, chemicals supplied as garden fertilizers.

We have deliberately omitted the use of Vitamin B_1 (Benerva tablets) at this stage as the alcohol content of the basic wine is sufficiently low to permit fermentation out to dryness without undue difficulty, but for the secondary fermentation the inclusion of Vitamin B_1 is desirable.

In order to weigh out reliably and accurately fractions of an ounce and small metric quantities, readers would find the Dr. Oetker 777 beam scale balance invaluable. This balance, originally imported specially from Germany for this book, is thoroughly recommended by us for use with all recipes (not only our own) which specify particular ingredients such as acids, di-ammonium phosphate and tannin in terms of weight; it will weigh up to 4 oz. (125 gm.), but is only obtainable from specialised suppliers.

SPARKLING PEACH

INGREDIENTS

Imperial	Metric	U.S.A.	
2½ lb.	1¼ kg.	2 lb.	Peaches, fresh, sound and ripe
1½ lb.	680 gm.	1⅛ lb.	White sugar (approx.)
0.17 oz.	5 gm.	0.14 oz.	Nutrient, ammonium phosphate
			Pectolytic enzyme to manufacturers instructions
½ oz.	15 gm.	½ oz.	Tartaric acid (approx.)
			Yeast champagne culture
0.07 oz.	2 gm.	0.05 oz.	Tannin (approx.)
2	2	2	Campden tablets
1 gal.	4½ l.	1 gal.	Volume

PREPARATION AND METHOD

Stone and crush peaches and steep in ¾ gallon cold water, to which has been added sodium metabisulphite, pectolytic enzyme and 1 level teaspoon of acid. Leave in well-covered container 2-3 days, stirring occasionally. Strain off pulp and adjust sugar to give S.G. 0.070 and acid to 4 p.p.t. Add tannin, ammonium phosphate and working yeast starter. Fit airlock and ferment at 18°-21°C. (65°-70°F.) to dryness. Rack and fine as normal procedure. Store in cool, dark position until required for second bottle fermentation. Follow text.

This recipe can be used for fresh apricots using same quantities of ingredients but check acidity carefully as it is higher than for peaches.

SPARKLING GRAPE

INGREDIENTS

Imperial	Metric	U.S.A.	
12 lb.	5½ kilo.	10 lb.	White grapes
			As required white sugar
2	2	2	Campden tablets (or 10 ml. of a 10% sulphite solution)
0.17 oz.	5 gm.	0.14 oz.	Nutrient, ammonium phosphate
0.07 oz.	2 gm.	0.05 oz.	Tannin
			Pectolytic enzyme to suppliers instructions
			Tartaric acid as required
			Yeast champagne culture
1 gal.	4½ l.	1 gal.	Volume

PREPARATION AND METHOD

Select sound, ripe grapes. De-stalk and thoroughly wash. Extract juice by most efficient method available, avoid crushing pips. Yield of juice will be approx. ¾ gallon. Check acid content and adjust to 4 p.p.t. Add sulphite solution and allow juice to settle 2-3 days in covered glass container. Siphon off sediment and take hydrometer reading and adjust with sugar syrup to S.G. 0.070 (average S.G. of grape juice is about 0.060). Add nutrient salts, tannin, pectolytic enzyme and activated yeast starter. Ferment in temperature 18°-21° C. (65°-70°F.) and let wine go dry. Rack off lees as soon as possible. Follow normal racking and clearing procedure, top up to minimise air space and store wine in cool, dark surroundings for minimum of 6 months. Taste and assess quality prior to proceeding with the secondary fermentation in bottle. See text.

SPARKLING APPLE

INGREDIENTS

Imperial	Metric	U.S.A.	
6 lb.	2¾ kilo.	5 lb.	Apples, ripe dessert

1 lb.	450 gm.	¾ lb.	Apples, cooking
½ lb.	230 gm.	½ lb.	Sultanas
2	2	2	Campden tablets
0.17 oz.	5 gm.	0.14 oz.	Nutrient, ammonium phosphate
1 lb.	450 gm.	¾ lb.	White sugar (approx.)
			Pectolytic enzyme to manufacturers instructions
			Yeast champagne culture
¼ oz.	7 gm.	¼ oz.	Tartaric acid (approx.)
1 gal.	4¼ litres	1 gal.	Volume

PREPARATION AND METHOD

Wash, core and crush apples, rinse and coarsely mince sultanas. Steep in 5 pints of cold water with sulphite and pectolytic enzyme. Strain and press after 2 days. Adjust with sugar syrup to S.G. 0.070 and with acid to 4 p.p.t. Add nutrient salts and activated yeast starter. Ferment to dryness, 18°-21°C. (65°-70°F.), rack and clear, and follow text. If a fuller flavour is desired, omit steeping period and ferment on pulp for 3 days.

COMMENTS

To prevent darkening of apple wine (oxidation) the minimum of 1 Campden tablet per gallon must be used after fermentation and containers must be kept full.

SPARKLING MEAD

INGREDIENTS

Imperial	Metric	U.S.A.	
4 lb.	2 kilo.	3½ lb.	Light clover honey (preferably English)
			White sugar, as required
0.17 oz.	5 gm.	0.14 oz.	Nutrient, ammonium phosphate
0.17 oz.	5 gm.	0.14 oz.	Nutrient, potassium phosphate
4	4	4	Fresh oranges
¾ oz.	25 gm.	¾ oz.	Tartaric acid (approx.)
			Yeast champagne culture
2	2	2	Campden tablets
2 gm.	2 gm.	2 gm.	Tannin
1 gal.	4½ l.	1 gal.	Volume

Heat honey and orange juice in ¾ gallon of water to 77° C. (170°F.) and hold this temperature for twenty minutes. Do not boil. When cool add nutrient salts, adjust S.G. to 0.070 and acid to 4 p.p.t., add yeast starter and ferment to dryness, 18°-21°C. (65°-70°F.), then follow text. Many variants of this wine can be made by using other honeys and fruit juices. Flavour should be delicate. Correct acid and nutrient quantities must be maintained to ensure sound fermentation.

SPARKLING STRAWBERRY

INGREDIENTS

Imperial	Metric	U.S.A.	
4 lb.	2 kilo.	3½ lb.	Strawberries (ripe and sound)
6 fl. oz.	175 ml.	5 fl. oz.	Rose-hip syrup
1 lb.	450 gm.	¾ lb.	White sugar
0.17 oz.	5 gm.	0.14 oz.	Nutrient, ammonium phosphate
0.07	2 gm.	0.05 oz.	Tannin (approx.)
			Pectolytic enzyme to suppliers instructions
1 oz.	30 gm.	¾ oz.	Tartaric acid (approx.)
2	2	2	Campden tablets
			Yeast champagne culture
1 gal.	4½ l.	1 gal.	Volume

PREPARATION AND METHOD

De-stalk and crush strawberries, steep in ¾ gallons cold water with sulphite solution, ½ oz. acid and pecto. Strain after 2-3 days, adjust with sugar to S.G. 0.070 an acid to 4 p.p.t. Add balance of ingredients and prepared starter yeast. Fit airlock and ferment to dryness, 18°-21°C. (65°-70°F.). Rack and finish as text.

COMMENTS

The character of this wine is greatly enhanced by being sweetened to taste either by a non-fermentable agent (sorbitol) prior to the secondary fermentation or by adding a *liqueur d'expedition* at the *dégorgement* stage. Its colour may be usefully brightened by the addition of a few dark red rose petals, say two blooms not too fragrant in perfume.

SPARKLING RHUBARB

Imperial	Metric	U.S.A.	
6 lb.	2 ¾ kilo.	5 lb.	Rhubarb
6 fl. oz.	175 ml.	5 fl. oz.	Rose-hip syrup
0.17 oz.	5 gm.	0.14 oz.	Nutrient, ammonium phosphate
2 lb.	1 kilo.	1 ¾ lb.	White sugar (approx.)
0.07 oz.	2 gm.	0.05 oz.	Tannin
			Yeast champagne culture
2	2	2	Campden tablets
			Tartaric acid, as necessary for acid adjustment
1 gal.	4½ l.	1 gal.	Volume

PREPARATION AND METHOD

Choose young rhubarb stalks (forced are best), trim well away from the leaves, well wash and either put through juice extractor or crush and press. Steep the crushed stalks in cold water with Campden tablets and strain after 3 days. The pulp from juice extractor can be rinsed through with cold water and re-strained. Add balance of ingredients, adjusting S.G. to 0.070 and acid to 4 p.p.t.

By using young tender stalks the oxalic acid content is low and the traditional treatment to remove it by using precipitated chalk is not necessary. Ferment to dryness, 18°-21° C. (65°-70° F.) and then follow text.

SPARKLING GOOSEBERRY

INGREDIENTS

Imperial	Metric	U.S.A.	
6 lb.	2 ¾ kilo.	5 lb.	Gooseberries, medium ripe
1 ¾ lb.	800 gm.	1½ lb.	White granulated sugar (approx.)
2	2	2	Campden tablets
			Tartaric acid, as necessary
0.17 oz.	5 gm.	0.14 oz.	di-Ammonium phosphate
0.07 oz.	2 gm.	0.05 oz.	Tannin
			Pectolytic enzyme to suppliers instructions
			Yeast champagne culture
1 gal.	4½ l.	1 gal.	Volume

METHOD

Wash berries and break up the fruit by using a mincer, electric juicer, or any other convenient means. "Topping and tailing" is not necessary. To the prepared fruit add 6 pints (3.4l) of *cold* water, 2 Campden tablets or 10 ml. of sulphite solution and pectolytic enzyme. Leave to infuse in covered container for 2 days with occasional stirring. Press-out or strain-off and allow to settle for 1 day. Siphon-off and adjust the sugar content to S.G. 1.070. If the resultant volume is less than 1 gallon (4½ l.) add cold water and re-adjust the S.G. Check acid content by the "titration method" and correct with tartaric acid to 4 p.p.t. or assess flavour-wise. Add tannin, nutrient salts and an active champagne yeast starter. Ferment out to dryness, temperature 18°-21°C. (65°-70°F.) and then follow the text.

COMMENTS

To increase the acidity, which is mainly due to malic acid, tartaric acid is desirable to provide the balance necessary.

However, when the second fermentation is conducted during the autumn in order to provide a rapidly processed sparkling wine for Christmas celebrations of the same year, it would be preferable to avoid tartaric and to use citric acid instead.

Sparkling wine, containing tartaric aid, that has not seen frosty conditions is prone to tartrate fall-out in the champagne bottles. Such a young wine, although *dégorged* early, would be a little "yeasty" on the nose, but nonetheless exciting. 6 lb. per gallon of fruit would be expected to provide the character for a sparkling wine, a supplement of grape juice concentrate would be unnecessary in the authors' opinion.

RHUBARB AND STRAWBERRY FOR 1 GALLON

INGREDIENTS

Imperial	Metric	U.S.A.	
1.6 lb.	725 gm.	1.3 lb.	Rhubarb (young stalks)
200 ml.	200 ml.	167 ml.	Apple juice
5 fl. oz.	147 ml.	4.3 fl. oz.	White grape concentrate
6 fl. oz.	165 ml.	4.8 fl. oz.	Tinned peach (fruit and juice)
3 oz.	80 gm.	2.3 oz.	Tinned guava
3 oz.	80 gm.	2.3 oz.	Tinned mango
4 oz.	115 gm.	3.3 oz.	Fresh strawberries
1.2 lb.	545 gm.	1 lb.	Sugar

There is enough tannin in the fruit skins for a white wine. The rhubarb should be frozen in chunks and thawed by covering with sulphited water overnight. Strain through a collander and squeeze lightly. Mash the tinned fruit and strawberries and add the rhubarb juice along with recommended amounts of nutrient and pectolytic enzyme. Add an active champagne starter and ferment on the pulp for two days. Strain, add the sugar and ferment to dryness. Rack, fine, etc.

This light refreshing sparkling wine, with complex bouquet and flavour, is excellent for picnics and patio lunches.

CHARDONNAY STYLE FOR 1 GALLON

INGREDIENTS

Imperial	Metric	U.S.A.	
20 fl. oz.	570 ml.	16.5 fl. oz.	White grape concentrate
1 litre	1 litre	83 ml.	Apple juice
4 oz.	114 gm.	3.3 oz.	Banana
12 oz.	340 gm.	10 oz.	Fresh mango
4 oz.	114 gm.	3.3 oz.	Fresh peach
2 oz.	57 gm.	1.7 oz.	Fresh or frozen strawberries
1 lb.	455 gm.	13.3 oz.	Sugar

Add an active champagne starter to the apple juice and grape concentrate in a volume of 96 fl. oz. imperial (80 fl. oz. USA). When fermenting well, pulp ferment with the mashed fruit and recommended additions of nutrient and pectolytic enzyme. After two days, strain off the pulp, add the sugar and ferment to dryness. Rack, fine, etc.

This 'Blanc de Blanc' has Chardonnay characteristics and always does well on the show bench.

A Medium Sweet Sparkling Rosé

A lively, refreshing sparkling rosé can be made from either of these two wines by sweetening, at the disgorgement stage, with raspberry juice. The raspberry juice is made by squeezing the juice from fresh or frozen raspberries, treating with a pectolytic enzyme, and allowing to clear. If necessary, the clarified juice may be filtered. When crystal

63

clear, sugar is stirred into the juice until it is saturated. This sweetened juice can be stored frozen in 40 ml aliquots until needed.

At the disgorgement stage, one aliquot of 40 ml. sweetened raspberry juice (pre-cooled to 0°C) is added to the disgorged wine along with any more wine needed to top up to within 2 inches of the stopper. After mixing, the wine can be served almost immediately with no ill effects from these operations. The wine will not, however, remain stable without sorbate treatment which is not recommended in this application. Wines made by this sweetening process, although perfectly safe and sound, should be used within one week of sweetening to avoid problems of possible refermentation.

This most refreshing sparkling rosé appears to suit most palates. The style has won first prize in National Show two years in a row and is always well received at tastings.

Temperature Aspect

The reason for specifying a temperature range of 18°C to 21°C for the initial fermentation of the recipes was conditioned to comply with an anticipated room temperature range existing throughout the year in a centrally heated and well insulated house, to support this temperature range for the must. The ideal temperature for fermenting white wine with Gervin Varietal C champagne yeast is 16°C and those readers who are able to control the temperature *downwards* would be wise to work near to that value. However, when the ambient temperature is unusually high a useful dodge is to cover the fermenting vessel with a continuously dampened cloth, in the shade outside, where a breeze is useful to assist the cooling effect. A temperature drop of as much as 5°C may be achieved by this method.

The recipes for Rhubarb and Strawberry and Chardonnay Style basic wines have been included by courtesy of the compiler, National judge, Bill Smith of High Wycombe.

CHAPTER 8

Racking, Clarification and Assessment

Racking

When fermentation is complete your wine will begin to clear and a fairly well defined layer of yeast and debris will slowly make its way to the base. The liquid above the layer will not be absolutely clear as it will contain suspended yeast cells and other matter. By the time no obvious layer of suspended matter is apparent the wine will be ready for the first "racking" from the *lees*. It is important to avoid letting the wine stand on the *lees* for a prolonged period as otherwise off-flavours may develop due to the decomposition of the dead yeast cells and other debris forming the sediment.

"Racking", as the process is called, is most conveniently carried out by using a siphon tube. The deposit in the container may be easily disturbed, so care should be exercised in moving the container prior to racking. The simple straight ended siphon tube, unless placed some distance from the lees, will tend to exert a "vacuum cleaner action" and draw up some of the deposit along with the wine. This defeats the purpose of racking and to enable you to remove the maximum volume of wine it is wise to employ a siphon tube which terminates in a "U" bend.

Avoiding Oxidation

This partially clear wine from the first racking should be run into another container of the same size and since a little of the wine will have to be left behind with the *lees,* topping-up of the new container to keep it full will be necessary. This making good of the *ullage* is most important to avoid *oxidation;* use some of the same wine saved for the purpose, or another wine of similar character.

Oxidation is characterised by the smell of acetaldehyde (part of the natural bouquet of sherry) and should on no account be allowed to develop in a base for sparkling wine, as an *oxidised* flavour here is quite unthinkable and completely out of character.

When no suitable topping up wine is available a rather ingenious scheme has been put forward by Dr. John Harrison, a friend of ours. He bores a blind hole in the bottom of the cork large enough to accommodate a Campden tablet. The hole is then plugged with cotton wool and as the vapour penetrates so it releases sulphur dioxide gas which forms a protective layer above the wine, without actually dissolving in it to any appreciable depth.

Wine must not touch the cork. Allow ullage 1″-2″

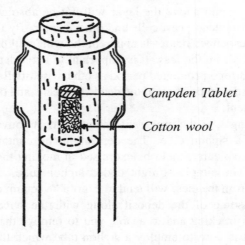

Campden Tablet

Cotton wool

With wines other than sherry it is usual to add a little sulphite following racking to "mop-up" the oxygen absorbed from the atmosphere during the process, but with sparkling wine bases it is important not to overdo the sulphite, for this could adversely affect the performance of the second fermentation in the closed bottle. The 100 p.p.m. of sulphite (2 Campden tablets per gallon) added at the must stage should be adequate to protect the wine against oxidation and bacterial infection right up to the second fermentation, with careful processing during the racking and clarification procedures.

Stoppering of the containers must be really effective and for this purpose we prefer to use sound natural corks (some rubber bungs are known to taint the wine) or polythene foil secured by tight-fitting rubber bands. This latter method has the advantage of permitting any residual gas pressure to escape, but will not readily admit oxygen from the atmosphere; in fact, it acts rather like a non-return valve. New wine, freshly racked, frequently contains some dissolved gas which may exert pressure on the stopper with a rise in temperature as the gas comes out of solution.

Tilly Timbrell, the well known exponent of wine cookery, has suggested a refinement to this method of capping the bottles, in which a cotton wool pad is sandwiched between two layers of polythene foil. A single layer of foil may easily become perforated by an accidental knock, but with the cushioning protection provided by the cotton wool, damage is almost impossible.

Second Racking

After the first racking a further sediment usually forms, composed mainly of dead and inactive yeast cells. To remove this it is usual to carry out a second racking within three to four weeks. As a champagne yeast culture has been employed for the initial fermentation, we frequently save some of this sediment together with the wine and store in a refrigerator in a small capped and completely filled bottle, for subsequent use in starting the second fermentation. Such yeast has already become acclimatised to the conditions of fermentation, to the ingredients used, and to the influence of sulphite, so it is usually excellent and reliable for starting the second fermentation. This is one reason we recommend the use of a champagne culture throughout the entire process.

Fining

Three months after the second racking the wine may have cleared completely and be star-bright, but sometimes despite careful processing it may exhibit some degree of *colloidal* haze, and this will require treatment — or *fining.* Although wines generally clear given time, there is nothing wrong with speeding the process by artificial means. Such a permanent suspension is composed of extremely small particles in constant agitation and all possess the same electrical charge.

Where the wine remains obstinately cloudy following the racking process and the haze is not of a *colloidal* nature, filtering can frequently solve the problem. Your authors do not advocate "open" filtering for delicate wines, owing to the very real danger of *oxidation.* We would recommend the use of the Southern Vineyard's **Vinbrite,** or the **Harris filter** supplied by Rogers (Mead) Ltd. Both operate on a closed system and minimise oxidation of the wine being filtered. Incidentally, a *colloidal haze* will not respond to conventional filtering; it generally requires a fining action to induce clarity.

Some hazes are caused by metal pick-up from utensils and by metallic sprays on fruit, but these are very rarely encountered in amateur spheres and require somewhat complex chemical treatment to effect their removal.

But, before taking any fining action, it is advisable to check for pectin (see page 39), and if present, treat accordingly with a pectolytic enzyme.

The normal fining medium in the champagne region is *isinglass,* a fish glue derived from the roes of certain sturgeon. This is preferred because of its relatively mild action on the wine quality. Where particularly stubborn hazes are encountered the more drastic gelatine-tannin combination has to be employed, but the resultant champagne may not be given vintage rating. Both these methods are somewhat complicated to carry out for the amateur and we would recommend the use of a proprietary fining agent which is considerably simpler to employ and reliable in action. Other agents are ex-blood, white of egg, casein and Bentonite.

It is virtually impossible to forecast with any certainty which fining agent will solve a particular haze problem and it is therefore wise to carry out pilot experiments before treating the main portion of the wine. Bentonite and Gervin finings have, in our experience, rarely failed to clear our own wines processed in recent years.

Using Bentonite

Like many fellow winemakers, we now favour the use of Bentonite, a powdered clay of volcanic origin. Be careful to purchase your supply from a reputable source. The genuine material is mined in Fort Benton, Wyoming, but Bentonite of doubtful origin may have an "earthy" flavour. We prefer to buy our own supply in 1 lb. (500 gm.) packs, which generally last through two seasons. Before using the purchase we carry out a "dummy run" with plain water to make absolutely certain that no off-flavours are likely to be bestowed upon the valuable basic wine.

Bentonite carries a negative charge, and is particularly useful in removing nitrogenous substances such as albumins and proteins from the wine which all have a positive charge.

Proteins can be particularly troublesome in young wines, as they are very sensitive to variations in temperature, in that a wine initially clear may develop a protein haze at a later stage, when bottled, and of course such an occurrence would naturally be most unwelcome. Normally, with adequate maturation in bulk, wines lose their proteins by precipitation long before bottling takes place; but where young wines are bottled early, as is generally the case with sparklers, Bentonite is most useful in providing the degree of stability required.

When dealing with a 5 gallon unit, the quantity of Bentonite (as recommended by the suppliers) is ¾ oz. (22 gm.); and this should be made up into a stiff paste with a little wine or water. The quantity required for 1 gallon units could be difficult to weigh out, so it is best to make up a stock suspension as described later. The preparation of the paste is sometimes a little difficult in that it is rather sticky and tends to adhere to the utensils employed. However, as the swelling power and consequent increase in volume is so great, if a little of the paste is lost it is of no real consequence.

The paste is allowed to stand for 24 hours before being dispersed in approximately ½ pint (250 ml.) of the wine. The most convenient way is to use an electric food mixer, but it can be done by hand. The fining mixture is then added to the bulk of the wine to be treated, with thorough and occasional stirring, especially during the first half-hour. Some air will have been introduced into the wine due to the violence of the electric mixing, but we find that no serious *oxidation* results.

When fining single gallons it is a good idea to make up a stock suspension from ¾ oz. (22 gms.) of Bentonite in ½ pint (250 ml.) of water to which is added 1 Campden tablet to maintain sterility and freshness.

If this ¾ oz. (22 gm.) of Bentonite is placed in a *dry* flat-bottomed standard size wine, or similar, bottle the powder may be incorporated in the water by occasional but energetic shaking during a 24 hour period, thus avoiding the need for mechanical mixing. A paper scale marked off in fifths and gummed in position is useful for measuring out the dosage required.

The disadvantage of using Bentonite is the rather heavy fall-out or wastage which can be as much as 2 inches in a 5 gallon bottle. Nevertheless, this sediment may be filtered, the wine being sulphited to offset oxidation, and used up as a still wine. Some winemakers, we hear, sucessfully re-use the spent Bentonite fall-out to clear other wines, but we have no personal experience of this technique.

Bentonite may be used to advantage in treating wines which have been over-fined by other agents, but must itself not be used in excess, otherwise an earthy flavour may develop. There is no advantage in "good measure" — ¾ oz. (22 gm.) per 5 gallons should not be exceeded. It will also cope with a haze resulting from iron pick-up, possibly from careless handling of rusty carboy cages or from unsound utensils.

Some readers may prefer the convenience of a prepared Bentonite gel, such as the one marketed by Rogers (Mead) Ltd called **Winefine.**

Having cleared the wine with Bentonite, allow it to stand for about four weeks to make quite sure that all the flocculent precipitate has fully settled out. On the rare occasions when Bentonite does not provide a perfectly limpid wine, the technique is to re-fine with a colloidal silica and gelatine combination, such as Gervin Two Part Finings.

In commerce it is not unusual to use a three stage fining process — particularly in Germany — to precede the bottling of young wines. This process relies upon Bentonite followed up by colloidal silica -and gelatine. In fact Gervin conforms to the latter combination, so we can easily utilise the commercial process. Such fining of commercial wines is always followed by closed system filtering to remove the last traces of fining agent; but as amateurs we can afford the time to wait until gravity has fulfilled the purpose.

Where tartaric acid has dominated in the basic wine it is advisable to chill it sufficiently to expel the cream of tartar, either by placing in a refrigerator set near freezing for, say two weeks, or to expose it to wintry conditions outside before attempting the second fermentation. Failure to do this may result in adherent crystals forming on the inner wall of the champagne bottle providing a problem remuage.

Assessing the Wine

Prior to the final fining operation it is prudent to assess the wine for flavour and general balance, since any adjustments made for acid and/or tannin can easily disturb the composition of the wine and cause hazes which will then require further treatment. To assess a wine at such an early age requires some degree of experience and a newcomer to sparkling wine techniques may feel inclined to call upon the advice from a more experienced winemaker, known to have a discerning palate. Much painstaking time and effort will go into the subsequent stages of the process and although the winemaker may feel confident to cope with the practical problems of *remuage* and *dégorgement* he may not be quite so sure about the suitability of the wine intended to be sparkled.

A winemaker without a palate is rather like a ship without a rudder and a newcomer to winemaking, who is ambitious, should take every possible opportunity to improve the education of his palate by tasting as many different wines as possible, whether they be commercial or amateur made.

Whenever going out to dinner in a restaurant or hotel, abroad or in this country, try to broaden your experience of commercial wine. Attend as many commercial wine tastings as you can, and take full advantage of the opportunities for gaining experience that your wine circle provides: offer your services as a steward to a judge at a club competition. In this way it is possible to taste the best wines made by your colleagues. Stewarding at the regional or national shows is an even better opportunity to educate the palate and most national judges are only too pleased to help a winemaker who shows keen and active interest. To make good sparkling wine only requires such an interest to be commensurate with a practical approach to winemaking.

We now should possess a perfectly limpid wine which may of course have cleared naturally and this will have been assessed in quality before proceeding with the second fermentation in a stoppered champagne bottle. Needless to say it must be brilliantly clear, for once bottled it is inconvenient to reach the contents for further treatment.

CHAPTER 9

Adjusting the Sugar Content

Having produced a clear and suitable wine we now have to ferment it further — in the bottle — to provide that delicious sparkle that we are after. We do this by adding a carefully controlled quantity of sugar in order to provide a safe working pressure of carbon dioxide. It is this dissolved gas that will supply the sparkle in the wine glass and the effervescence as it escapes from the wine.

The basic wine may well have come from your cellar (if it meets the critical standards counselled in Chapter 6), it may have been made from one of our well-tried recipes in Chapter 7, or perhaps you may have blended suitable wines to provide a well-balanced cuvée. In the last case, the newly-mixed wines *must* be allowed to rest for a few weeks in order to ensure that the resultant wine is completely stable, that it has not developed a haze, as sometimes occurs. Should a blended wine prove unstable, it is necessary to fine and rack before proceeding with the second fermentation.

The amount of sugar must be carefully controlled to ensure a sufficiently exciting sparkle and effervescence, but on the other hand limited so that not too much gas pressure is developed, as otherwise there would be a danger from fracture due to an excessive force exerted upon the bottle. Champagne is usually fermented in the bottle to a pressure in the region of 90 lb. per square inch as measured at cellar temperature 10°C. (50°F.). For temperatures below this ambient the pressure would be correspondingly lower and when stored in a hotter atmosphere it could rise to as much as 120 lb. p.s.i.

It is most unwise for amateurs to aim at such a high working pressure for fear of bottle breakage and consequent personal injury. In the

Champagne district they usually re-ferment the wine prepared from the cuvée with 2.4% sugar present (approx. 4 oz. per gallon) and there they are using new bottles but we shall, in all probability, be using second-hand ones.

Once a champagne bottle has been maintained at high pressure for a number of years it is prone to develop a weakness on re-pressurising, according to the bottle manufacturers. In fact, the commercial sparkling winemakers would not entertain the use of second-hand bottles (above ¼ sizes), whether for champagne or wine made by the *cuve close* method.

This being so, clearly our only safe solution is to work at a lower pressure than used commercially. We are convinced that the pressure should rarely be allowed to exceed 55 lb. p.s.i., as derived from 1⅝% sugar; then the danger of bottle fracture is reduced to a minimum. Even so, remember that the bottles must be selected to be free from scratches and blemishes.

Readers should in no way feel cheated by this advice, for there is a well-known champagne called "Crémant" which possesses about half the "fizz" of the classic version, but it might be considered *infra dig.* to steal the name!

Any attempt to exceed our recommended sugar levels most definitely calls for a face-shield, strong gloves and heavy clothing for subsequent handling of the bottles, prior to disgorgement.

Testing for Sugar

If we are to be so precise, it is obviously essential to know how much residual sugar is present in the basic wine before attempting to build up the level required for the secondary fermentation.

The method, sometimes suggested, of bottling an already fermenting wine, is not to be recommended. The wine can very well end up cloudy and lacking in effervescence, or on the other hand it can develop a dangerously high gas pressure with consequential explosive tendencies!

Tasting the wine to check for sugar is not very meaningful, as with the high acid content (4 p.p.t.), even 2% of residual sugar, composed almost entirely of glucose and fructose, would be difficult to detect on the palate.

An accurate specific gravity measurement is convenient in assessing the sugar content, but the ideal way is to combine this with chemical analysis by means of a Clinitest kit. No knowledge of chemistry is required! Diabetics use this simple kit to check the sugar present in their urine— a liquid hardly akin to wine! It was Acton and Duncan who some years ago grasped the significance of its usefulness in solving our particular problem.

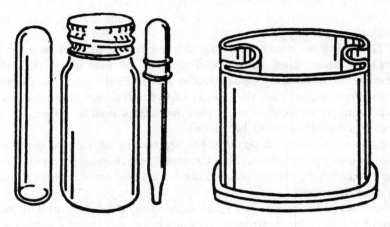

The Clinitest Kit

The Clinitest, available from most pharmacists, retails at £2.86 (at the time of going to press). It is simple enough to use, will record sugar content up to 2% (which is high enough) and is sufficiently accurate for our sparkling wines. It is based upon Benedicts method for sugar determination. The kit contains explicit instructions which should be followed faithfully, but instead of using urine you will be testing wine!

The Clinitest only indicates inverted and other reducing sugars, accurately. Invert sugar and glucose both respond in truthful fashion, but the test is *not* suitable for household granulated sugar (sucrose), so it is useless to apply the test to a finished wine that has had household sugar added to it *recently*. In such a case it could return zero sugar. Although household sugar has been recommended for the basic wine, for its fermentation, it will become converted into inverted sugar during the fermentation by a yeast *enzyme* called *invertase*. Then, any residual sugar would be expected to respond to the Clinitest, correctly.

Incidentally, there should be no problem, at all, in fermenting out the basic wine to dryness, i.e. green on the Clinitest chart, when working with such a low specific gravity of 1.070, as specified, and a well nourished must.

It now remains to dissolve household sugar in the basic wine to a concentration of 1.5%. This amounts to 2.4 oz. (68 g) per gallon. American readers would need to add 56.8 g to one of their gallons. However, should the Clinitest have indicated say ¼ % of sugar then, you will require less to add, in fact, only 2 oz. per gallon. Newcomers to the sparkling wine and the Clinitest would be advised to use wines exhibiting the green end of the chart which records the lowest possible sugar contents. Experience has shown that the colour of rosé and *light* red wines has no appreciable effect upon the accuracy of the test.

The Specific Gravity Method

As we have mentioned earlier, we do not recommend the bottling of an uncontrolled fermenting must even when its specific gravity falls to a particular value, as the value we put forward, with sugar addition, depends upon starting the basic wine at S.G. 1.070, a value generally lower than in still winemaking. This value *is critical* to the process. Indeed, we recommend the addition of sugar, to a fully fermented bone dry basic wine, to the value of S.G. 1.000 — the magic value. But, if the temperature of the wine departs significantly from that specified on the hydrometer scale you would be advised to apply a correction by using the table on page 42. Alternatively, you could adjust the temperature of the wine to suit the one specified on the scale. This method, we would point out, is not quite as accurate as adding a controlled quantity of sugar to a known volume of bone dry wine and does, in fact, call for the use of a narrow range laboratory-style hydrometer. Hydrometers, normally available to the amateur winemaker, have rather cramped graduations on the scale and are consequently difficult to read with sufficient accuracy, but entirely adequate for other purposes. Narrow range hydrometers are currently obtainable from Vigo Vineyard Supplies for the more dedicated sparkling winemaker. We use the .950 to 1.000 range which, incidentally, will read to 1.005. In both the previous and specific gravity methods it is an advantage to use caster sugar as this dissolves more readily. Of course with the specific gravity method the precise volume of wine being adjusted need not be known, but the sugar must be added carefully by trial and error, to avoid overshooting the S.G. 1.000 mark.

Vigo Vineyard Supplies
Bollhayes Park
Clayhidon
Cullompton
Devon
Tel: 0823 680 230

Authors' Note: Diabetics, who currently use either the Clinistix or Reflolux S systems, could find that either would indicate the absence of inverted sugar in the finished basic wine, but they must not be relied upon for quantitative measurement as the systems are designed to function in a less acid environment than found with wine.

76

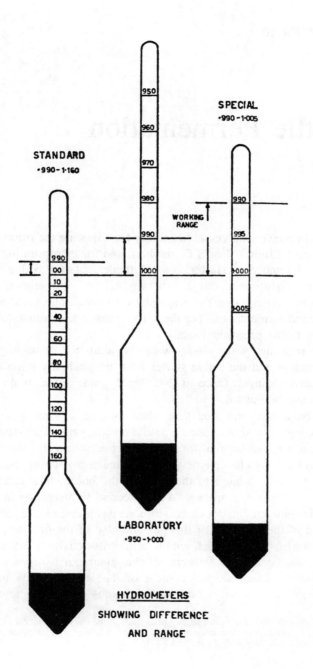

HYDROMETERS

SHOWING DIFFERENCE

AND RANGE

CHAPTER 10

Bottle Fermentation

The most convenient vessel to employ for adjusting the sugar content by either the "Clinitest" or S.G. method, and for incorporating additional vitamin B_1 and yeast starter, is a polythene container with a well-fitting lid. The disturbance due to stirring in the sugar should introduce sufficient oxygen from the atmosphere to encourage yeast activity for the second fermentation, but the active yeast starter must not be added directly to the prepared wine.

Refermenting your basic wine is akin to re-starting a stuck fermentation and the active starter must be gradually introduced to its new surroundings. Once it has "got going" the wine can with confidence be bottled.

We have recommended that when making a wine specifically for "sparkling" one should use a true champagne yeast right from the start. Whilst it may not be vital for the first fermentation, for the second one it certainly is. A champagne yeast is granular and dense, and therefore will not readily adhere to the sides of the bottle, thus facilitating the subsequent *remuage* process. As the second fermentation in the closed bottle is conducted under carbon dioxide gas pressure, the yeast must be tolerant of the presence of this gas and also of the pressure developed in the bottle, both of which tend to inhibit its activity. Furthermore, the yeast must be able to ferment all the sugar out to dryness at a low temperature, to an alcohol content of the order of 13% under these conditions if necessary; but we would not expect the level actually

Authors' Note: With today's champagne yeasts, such as the Gervin Varietal C, it is not always necessary to induce the fermentation in stages, in fact, the direct addition of supermarket grape juice starter could very well do the trick.

produced to be greater than 12%. Finally, the yeast must be a good bouquet-former since the wine, after fermentation should preferably spend at least one year on the yeast sediment and could well benefit from longer exposure.

It is best to prepare your yeast starter some 3 days in advance (as described in Chapter 6, for the basic wine). A fresh champagne culture can very well be employed, but sediment from a disgorged bottle from the previous year can also be used, especially one that has yielded well to *remuage*, where the yeast came away easily from the sides of the botte.

Nutrients

Sufficient mineral nutrient salts should remain from the first fermentation, but it is a good idea to provide additional vitamin B_1, by dividing a 25 mg tablet in quarters and to add one quarter to each gallon. We would not recommend the unreserved use of yeast energisers, unless the preparation employed is known by experience to produce a clean wine, one free from off-flavours and unusual scents. Some yeast energisers have an adverse effect upon the quality of wine, especially when used in excess.

Glycerine

Where a dry sparkling wine is envisaged, we invariably add ½ fl. oz. (15 ml.) of B.P. glycerine per gallon to the base wine. This gives a degree of smoothness which helps to temper the edge of dryness, but it should not be used in excess or a cloying flavour will result. In fact, a dry sparkling wine thus treated invariably has a wide appeal, to the educated palate as well as to the occasional drinker. Without additional sweetening the glycerine provides a *brut* character to the wine.

The Yeast Starter

Having made these adjustments, add an equal volume of the prepared wine to the active starter, which should be 5% of the volume of wine being treated (8 fl. oz. for 1 gallon) and store in warm surroundings, preferably near to 20°C (68°F). When fermenting vigorously the volume is doubled by a further addition of the prepared wine. Once this augmented starter is fully active it is then added to the main portion, whose temperature has also been increased to about 20°C. (68°F.) and stirred in thoroughly. This starter may be made up from supermarket white grape juice which has much the same specific gravity as the basic wine, so will not upset the balance. The lid is fitted to the container and a watch is kept for activity, which may not begin for some three or four days. As soon as bubbles begin to break on the surface the wine will be ready for bottling.

Some writers advocate bottling the wine as soon as the starter is added, but we prefer to make aboslutely certain that fermentation is active before proceeding to fill the champagne bottles.

Sometimes the second fermentation has to be encouraged by additional aeration, and needless to say this is far more conveniently carried out prior to bottling. Additional aeration is best carried out by pouring the wine from one vessel to another with an exaggerated splashing action.

The bottles must not be filled completely and a head space should be left between the base of the stopper and the wine. This provides a reservoir of gas which acts as a propellant charge to drive out the frozen yeast slug and cork when disgorging. **We recommend 1½ in. to 2 in. of head space.** Although the wine will be pressurised at this stage, it would take a finite time for the gas to come out of solution in order to provide sufficient energy to release a particularly well-fitting stopper, without the head space. Furthermore, this somewhat generous head-space reduces the loss of wine due to the effervescence caused by the sudden release of the pressure. When bottling it is a good idea to fill at the same time a screw-capped 1-pint beer bottle. This can then be used as a test bottle; its stopper can be gently released at times during the second fermentation to assess the progress by gauging the degree of pressure generated.

The polythene stoppers, of course, must be wired into position with the wire hoods to prevent the gas pressure blowing them out; crown corks are self-sufficient.

In order to encourage the fermentation, the champagne bottles should be stored horizontally in warm surroundings at much about the same temperature as recommended for the addition of the starter, at least for the first week. From then onwards it is desirable to store the wine under slightly cooler conditions and this procedure is discussed in Chapter 11, which deals exclusively with maturing.

Maturing

Temperature Control

Your newly-bottled wine should be stored for the first week in warm surroundings (about 18°C., 65°F.) in order to encourage the early stages of the secondary fermentation, but when fermentation is under way it should be transferred, if possible, to slightly cooler conditions. A cellar temperature near 12°C. (54°F.) is ideal.

Few winemakers are fortunate enough to have such facilities at their disposal to provide the desirable slow and steady fermentation which ensues under these conditions, but there is no need to be unduly concerned, for we have made perfectly sound sparkling wine which has been subjected to very variable temperature conditions considerably in excess of 12°C. (54°F) (in garages and out-houses). Many of our sparkling wines — made under conditions far removed from the ideal — have received favourable comment from commercial and amateur tasters alike and have also won awards at major amateur wine shows, but this is not to say that the wine might not have been even better had it matured under much cooler conditions! Amateur sparkling wine production is at present in its infancy, but as time goes on standards will become more demanding, and will call for greater care in processing.

The temperature should not exceed 25°C (77°F.) for lengthy periods and we would endeavour — as far as is possible — to avoid high temperatures and rapid fluctuations. A slow and steady fermentation will give better bubble retention in the finished wine.

When working with fresh fruit one normally ferments the basic wine during the summer or autumn, exposes it to the cold of winter, and has it clear by early spring; so it should not be unduly difficult to exercise the requisite degree of control over temperature during the secondary fermentation stage in the following year.

The bottles, either sealed with polythene stoppers wired in position, or by 29 mm. crown cork closures, must be resting in a horizontal position, stoppers outward, and as pressure will be developed in the bottles as fermentation proceeds, they should be handled carefully. Should handling be necessary, hold the bottles by the neck (the strongest part) at arm's length and, away from the face. If our instructions concerning sugar levels are followed we do not anticipate dangers due to bottle fracture; but readers who operate on a substantial scale may feel inclined to invest in a face-shield when handling pressurised bottles. Suitable face-shields may be obtained by mail-order from Chubb Panorama Limited.*

We do not consider sparkling wine making made by our process as any more hazardous than beer making and, provided that our recommendations are followed, there should certainly be no unfortunate incidents. These recommendations have been given in good faith and are based upon some years of experience, but obviously we cannot accept responsibility for mishaps during processing which is not under our direct control. There is always the remote possibility of an unnoticed flaw in a bottle which could cause a weakness, or excessive pressure could be built up by mis-reading the Clinitest or hydrometer scale when adjusting the sugar content for the secondary fermentation.

We find it convenient to use one-litre size cardboard wine bottle crates for storing the bottles or, alternatively, the Italian sparkling-wine ones, as the special design of most of the French champagne box containers does not lend itself to carrying out the twisting action demanded when shaking down the yeast. Storing the wine in cardboard-box crates also protects it from the prolonged effect of daylight which, it is thought, could spoil the quality of the wine despite the dark colour of the bottles. Although the standard champagne bottle has much about the same capacity as the still wine bottle, due to its heavier wall thickness it will not go happily into the more common cardboard wine bottle crate.

Bottles are best stored in the horizontal position to provide maximum contact of the wine with the thick line of yeast which forms along the length of the bottle during the secondary fermentation. Sparkling wine gains much of its character by contact with the special champagne yeast

* Model M507/2 (replaces the one shown). Supplier: Chubb Panorama Limited, Evans Place, Industrial Estate, Bognor Regis, West Sussex. Tel. 0243 828911.

82

and baker's yeast or brewer's yeast are certainly not likely to make an acceptable sparkling wine.

It is desirable to mature the wine on the yeast deposit for at least one year and during this period complex chemical changes take place. The young wine becomes progessively smoother and develops a pleasant bouquet as well as flavour. Substances — called amino-acids — are released from the yeast sediment and modern opinion is that these amino-acids have a greater effect upon the development of the bouquet than does the ester formation due to the reaction between the acids and alcohols present in the wine. Traces of other alcohols, besides ethyl alcohol (ehtanol), are formed during fermentation, and the interaction and marrying-up of the trace and major components is an exceedingly complex process; but the final result, when adequate time is allowed to mature, is well worth the patience.

Most of us have to improvise a wine cellar or storage. Some of the more enthusiastic winemakers have dug their own small cellars, sometimes under the garden shed or outhouse, which is used as the winery. Other colleagues of ours, with older houses — which have a considerable distance between the floorboards and ground level — have made trap doors and extended the depth to make for more comfortable access. To shield the wine from the effects of draughts is important, but naturally one must not impede the ventilation or there might be danger of dry rot to the wooden structure of the house.

Some winemakers, of course, are far more restricted and must look for the most even-temperatured place in the house or dwelling; usually the cupboard under the stairs will provide suitable cellar accommodation.

During the period of maturation it is a good plan to "rouse" (shake thoroughly) the sediment occasionally so that it re-settles in a different position in the horizontally placed bottle, an important stage of the process practised in the Champagne, but frequently overlooked by amateurs. This procedure breaks up the strata of sediment and makes for easier removal of the yeast later. In fact, the omission may sometimes result in a scum formation on the glass, which is often very difficult, or even impossible, to remove. Needless to say, the consequent disturbance to the wine will cause the release of some of the dissolved carbon dioxide gas and will of course increase the pressure exerted upon the bottle; however, this operation may be performed quite conveniently without fully withdrawing the bottles from their cardboard crate, should these be of a rugged construction.

CHAPTER 12

Shaking Down the Yeast

We now come to the most interesting phase of sparkling wine production, that of shaking down the yeast on to the stopper (the "remuage" of champagne).

When the wine has been resting on the yeast sediment preferably for a year, this somewhat tedious process may begin. Incidentally, this sediment may contain — besides dead and inactive yeast cells — tartrates and other insoluble nitrogenous matter.

A newcomer to the sparkling wine "scene" may, if he wishes, avoid this process until more experience has been gained. It is always hard to resist the temptation to see how things are going, and one solution is to curtail the maturation period to about three months from the start of the secondary fermentation. At that time "rouse" at least one of the bottles to dislodge the horizontal formation of yeast sediment, stand the bottle upright, and the deposit will re-form on its base. In about three weeks you should have a bottle of clear sparkling wine (though with a yeast sediment), providing of course that the wine was properly fined in the first instance.

When the full champagne method is followed, it takes considerably longer to clear the wine because the conical shape of the neck of the inverted bottle impedes settlement by causing yeast to collect on its sloping sides. But when the bottle is stood upright, the parallel bottle sides offer very little resistance to a relatively quick fall out.

Although such a youthful wine will be a little "yeasty" on both palate and nose, there should be a sparkle and a gay effervescence. Chill the wine and with careful decanting to avoid disturbing the sediment, five or even six glasses may be dispensed before introducing any cloudiness into the poured wine. All the glasses must be poured in succession, for once the bottle is put down the wine will almost certainly become cloudy. We can assure our readers that with the thrill of tasting one's first sparkling wine, the slight yeastiness will be of little significance.

Many experienced sparkling wine makers avoid shaking the yeast down on to the stopper for home consumption, following the full term of horizontal maturing. In any case, a lively wine calls for careful decanting into the glasses to prevent an overflow from the foam produced by the effervescence.

On maturing, the yeasty bouquet and flavour should disappear entirely, despite the fact that the wine may have been permitted to remain on its sediment for several years and could well improve during this time. Most still wines, on the other hand, would suffer in quality as a result of such a prolonged exposure to a heavy yeast deposit, so we can only conclude that it is the presence of the carbon dioxide gas under pressure and the use of a special champagne yeast at the outset which preserves and enhances the character of a sparkling wine, made by the *méthod champenoise.*

When the sparkling wine is required to travel, either to a wine show or to a special occasion, the yeast sediment must be removed from the bottle as movement during the journey could well cause a disturbance and "cloud up" what was once a perfectly limpid wine above the sediment. A heavy sediment would almost certainly lose many points in competition, so wine for showing must have its yeast deposit removed. When dispensing a fully processed sparkling wine, it is rather nice to be able to invert the bottle completely on filling the last glass, to prove to the onlookers that the wine is brilliantly clear right to the end. Even with disgorged bottles, neither of us would dare to be so bold every time!

Shaking the yeast sediment down onto the stopper ("remuage") is quite tricky; to remove the very last traces of sediment requires skill, especially when dealing with the more difficult batches. Even the professionals have their "problem" remuages!

When the wine has sufficiently matured in its horizontal position "rouse" it once more to disperse the sediment, which should have formed a heavy layer along the length of the bottle. These "roused" bottles are then returned to the crate, this time with the punts facing outwards and a splash of light coloured emulsion paint or some other convenient marker applied at the 6 o'clock position.

When the bottles have rested for about three weeks the shaking down process may begin. The crates should be angled at approximately 45°, the bottles being inverted with their stoppers facing downwards. This can be done by propping up the crate with blocks of wood or by some other, possibly more sophisticated, means. No doubt the more keen sparkling wine maker will be anxious to construct a copy of a French pattern *pupitre,* as illustrated; it certainly makes for easier processing.

It now remains to encourage the sediment from the "roused" wine to gravitate towards the stopper. This usually takes about two months, but could be longer in more difficult cases. The procedure of twisting is then begun, and performed every other day. The bottles, in turn, are held firmly with fingers and thumb, and are withdrawn partially from the housings of the crate to be oscillated by gentle twisting action, first one way and then the other. On replacing, each bottle is then rotated onwards about one-eighth of a turn. The degree of rotation may be gauged by the marker on the punt.

The process depends for its effectiveness upon the cohesion of the lighter (less dense) particles comprising the sediment to the heavier ones, in order that the former may be given assistance on the downward journey towards the stopper. It follows, then, that the oscillations due to the twisting action must not be too violent, or these light particles will rise up and form a dispersion in the wine. Then much of the effort is in vain.

The purpose of the twisting movement is to detach the sediment from the glass and the cumulative action of twisting and rotating will gradually induce it to make its way downwards towards the stopper. After about two weeks the intervals between twistings may be lengthened and towards the end of the process the assembly of bottle and crate should be eased towards the vertical position by re-positioning the blocks or supporting mechanism.

It has been found by experience over many years that positioning at 45° and consequent twisting and rotating is usually best, but inverted bottles stood vertically at the outset sometimes respond quite well, especially when subjected to some form of vibration.

There will almost certainly be a great temptation to examine the bottles for progress by holding them up to a light directly in front of the face. Provided that a face-shield is worn, there is nothing wrong with this, but when one is not available some other effective transparent protective screen should be used just in case of accident. Twisting, unlike "rousing", does not release much carbon dioxide gas, so the

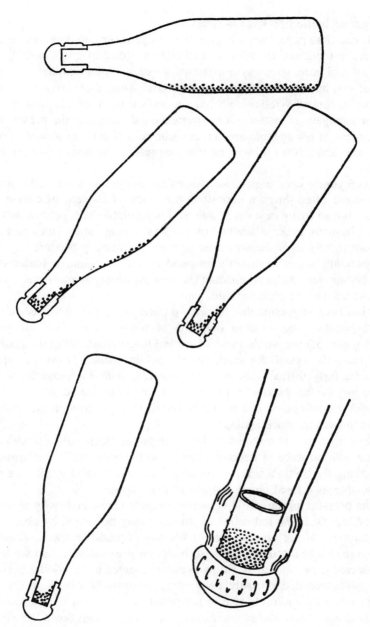

How the yeast is gradually shaken down on to the stopper, ready for disgorging

danger of bottle breakage is remote.

A true champagne yeast is granular in character and does not readily adhere to the glass (not all yeasts labelled as "champagne" may be true to type and pure, so always purchase the yeast from a reputable source); but if you have re-fermented a young basic wine, there may be present in the sediment a relatively high proportion of insoluble protein and other nitrogenous matter. Our experience indicates that the presence of an excess of nitrogenous matter can lead to difficulty in shaking down the yeast and it is for this reason that we prefer to Bentonite-fine the base wine.

Even young wine which has cleared naturally and is perfectly limpid may quite often throw a deposit in the bottle. This can, of course, be yeast, but in many cases it is due to this insoluble nitrogenous matter. The Germans make a feature of bottling young, still wines and are known to rely upon Bentonite as part of the fining procedure.

Sparkling wines invariably respond better to *remuage* under cold conditions, so it helps to conduct the process during winter-time, and it would be wise to plan for this.

It has been suggested that the incorporation of some well-washed fine silver sand in the wine at the time of bottling may facilitate yeast settlement, but we would expect the sand to gravitate out quite quickly, as do tartrate crystals for grape-based sparkling wines. However, where a particularly difficult batch is encountered, where a yeast deposit is adhering to the glass, "rousing" with the sand could no doubt be helpful, but of course one would be required to go through the shaking down procedure once again.

Shaking down is complete when one has a clear sight through the bottle with no trace of deposit adhering to the glass wall. Confirm this by giving the bottle a sharp twist; if sediment is present it will rise and be visible as a local cloud just above the stopper.

The pressure in the bottle is increased quite considerably by elevated temperatures. Some indication of pressure may be gained by observing the tautness of the muselet wires. We have found that the increase in pressure due to a temperature rise is not easy to calculate, so we have conducted experiments by fitting pressure gauges to individual bottles. We have recorded pressure rises of approximately 2½ lb. p.s.i. for every degree Centigrade rise in temperature.

There are other, less conventional, ways of shaking down the yeast. In *Wine Growing in England,* published some years ago, George Ordish

88

reported that he inverted his champagne bottles and relied upon the vibration of the heavy traffic which passed his house. This caused the cellar to oscillate to some extent and did the job for him automatically! Perhaps he was fortunate in having had a particularly responsive yeast which aided the process.

A development of this idea is to construct a partitioned crate made from a greengrocer's wooden market box as illustrated, load it with sparkling wine, and give this a ride in the boot of the car during winter months with the rear tyres pumped up a little above maker's recommended pressures. It is unwise to use this method during the summer-time when high temperatures can lead to an undesirable pressure building up in the bottles.

Poorly surfaced roads can be an advantage, but even with city roads one has to learn to live with a constant rattle coming from the rear of the car! In rear-engined cars travelling might be somewhat uncomfortable with high pressurised front tyres.

This method has been quite promising with easier batches, but the more difficult ones do require aid by occasional twisting. When winter comes around again the next phase in development is to set the wooden crate at 45°, possibly on undamped springs. Incidentally, it is important to allow freedom for movement of the bottle, hence the specially converted crate. Cardboad containers are very much quieter, but are unlikely to provide sufficient activity for the process. Should the occasion arise there is always scope for an emergency disgorging!

In the United States some commercial sparkling winemakers shake down the sediment by vibrating the champagne bottles, contained in specially designed crates, with the aid of a fork-lift—we claim no originality in the use of the internal combustion engine!

Postcript. The springs were not necessary but the oblique orientation has indeed speeded up the process time, and we have observed that the bottles rotate as well as vibrate in the housings of the wooden box.

CHAPTER 13

Disgorging and Sweetening

Disgorging (*dégorgement*) is the name given to the process of removing the temporary stopper along with the yeast sediment from the bottle after shaking down the yeast.

There is a way of avoiding both processes, if one cares to "cheat" a little! It entails using two bottles which have been allowed to lie for an adequate time for the sediment of yeast to have formed along their sides. After a thorough "rousing" (keep the bottles away from the face) these bottles are allowed to rest the normal way up until a firm deposit has been formed on the base. In about three weeks the wine above the sediment *should* be star-bright.

Both bottles, along with an empty one, are placed in a domestic refrigerator, the temperature of which has been adjusted to near the freezing-point of the wine, —4° C. (25°F.) With the drop in temperature the carbon dioxide gas becomes more soluble (bound-up in the wine) and consequently only a little is lost in subsequent operations. The contents should be adequately cooled in about one hour. It now remains to remove the stoppers in turn and to decant carefully (to minimise loss of gas) half the contents of each to the empty one. The bottles containing sediment are also combined, so that the final result is one bottle completely clear and another with a double dose of sediment. The clear one may be used for a special occasion or wine competition and the other to provide a wine for "home" consumption. Do not use two different wines or a haze may result. This simple method is commended to the newcomers of the craft.

If you decide to do the job properly and disgorge the yeast sediment in professional style the task is simplified if you own a suitable deep-

Don Hebbs using the "pupitre" presented to him and John Restall by Moussec Ltd.

A suitable crate for "mobile remuage:" shaking down the yeast by means of trips in the boot of a car

John Restall examines progress of a "mobile remuage"

Your authors salute you

Bottles chilling prior to disgorgement

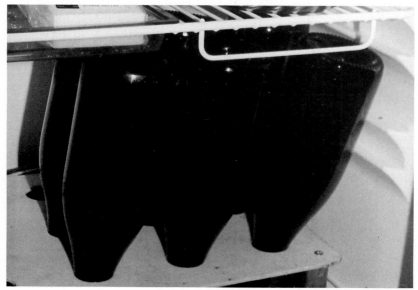

freeze unit — one that will accommodate an upturned bottle. No preliminary cooling is required, and should experience show that in your case the general cooling causes too great a reduction in pressure to blow out the ice slug, particularly where crown closures are used, it will help to lag all but the necks of the bottles with newspaper.

Deep freezers are invariably temperature controlled at about —18°C. —0.4°F.) and an ice slug in the neck usually forms in about 30 minutes, but the exact time may vary according to particular conditions.

Examine the inverted bottles periodically so as to avoid the formation of too long a slug of ice, which will make the hollow polythene stopper difficult to remove. With crown closures the ice slug should not be in excess of 1 inch, and with polythene stoppers need only just be proud of the end. Once the ice plug is formed the procedure is as for the freezing mixture method. This can be used where no deep-freeze is available and is in fact the traditional process.

The whole contents of the bottles must not be allowed to freeze for fear of bottle fracture. Furthermore, the bottles must not be gripped by the bare hand to avoid thermal shock — use a glove or napkin.

In following the classic method a chilling period of, say, one hour in a domestic refrigerator set at about 2°C. (36°F.) is needed to reduce the gas pressure and make for more easily controllable processing. When a refrigerator is not available the bottles may be chilled in a bucket of iced water.

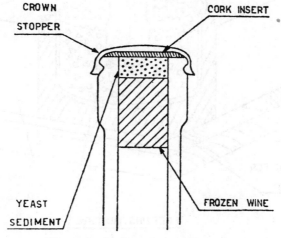

CROWN STOPPER

CORK INSERT

YEAST SEDIMENT

FROZEN WINE

Encapsulated sediment prior to disgorging

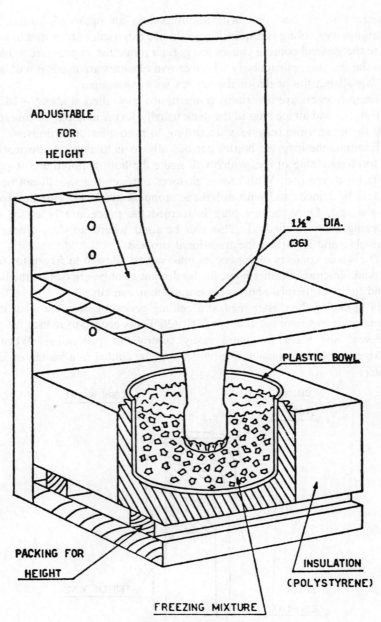

ADJUSTABLE
FOR
HEIGHT

1½" DIA.
(36)

PLASTIC BOWL

PACKING FOR
HEIGHT

INSULATION
(POLYSTYRENE)

FREEZING MIXTURE

Useful assembly for freezing bottle necks

The necks of the bottles have then to be frozen in a freezing mixture and a simple rack is useful for gauging the depth of immersion (as illustrated).

When cooking salt is scattered over an icy surface the effect is to melt the ice. It is more usual to associate melting only with the application of heat; but it would be wrong to do so in this particular instance, as the slush that forms actually becomes colder due to a complex physical change. The exact theory is beyond the scope of this book, but it is this phenomenon that we utilise in compounding the freezing mixture to encapsulate the yeast sediment to make disgorging easier.

A freezing mixture composed of 3 parts cooking salt and 10 parts snow or crushed ice is the most convenient to use and may be placed in a small plastic container. This composition should provide a temperature of approximately $-21\,°C.$ $(-5.8\,°F.)$ and although the exact quantities only will provide the minimum temperature, the actual composition is not very critical. It is far more important that the ice be well crushed into small pieces. Ice scrapings from the freezer or the refrigerator may be used in place of snow and of course this would be finely divided.

Various Freezing Mixtures

Sodium chloride (common salt)	33 parts	Snow	100 parts	$-21.3\,°C.$
Hydrated calcium chloride	10 parts	Snow	7 parts	$-54.9\,°C.$
Alcohol (meth. spirit)	77 parts	Snow	73 parts	$-30\,°C.$
Alcohol (meth. spirit)	Solid CO_2			$-72\,°C.$

Note: Finely divided ice may be used in place of the snow.

Usually it takes about 7 minutes to freeze the wine in the neck to completely encapsulate the yeast sediment and the progress may be observed by occasionally withdrawing the neck from the freezing mixture.

When polythene stoppers are used (we have recommended the hollow-centred type for the secondary fermentation) the ice should be allowed to form just above the end of the stopper. However, when enclosed polythene stoppers or crown closures are employed, the ice should be allowed to develop for about 1 inch above the stopper.

This ice invariably contains a slush-like core, due to the alcohol in the wine, and must be allowed to develop to an adequate overall length to provide sufficient strength for its fully effective removal. The ice slug is not hard, like that formed on a pond during a hard winter, but has a consistency similar to that of a water-based ice-cream. This allows it to be free from irregularities in the shape forming the neck of the bottle. The necks of champagne bottles are usually slightly tapered.

The ice-slug formed, the bottle is upturned to the normal position and the surplus salt washed away — otherwise it could contaminate the wine on fitting the fresh stopper. This should have been previously selected to ensure a good fit. The muselet wires should now be released by untwisting the loop and the pressure taken by holding the stopper in position by hand. When hollow-centered polythene stoppers are used they may be gradually eased out, for all the sediment will be contained in the cavity. This avoids a sudden release of pressure which sometimes causes an overflowing due to the effervescence. Where the enclosed stoppers or crown closures are concerned the technique is slightly different; in this case it is better to cant the bottle slightly and actually let the stopper or crown cork fly out. This operation is somewhat "messy" as the violence of the release leads to a "splattering" of both yeast sediment and ice, so should be aimed into a strategically placed bucket, or suitable container. Should the effervescence cause an overflow, the exit should be sealed by a well-placed thumb or bottle sealer* until the new stopper is fitted.

With the hollow-centred polythene stoppers disgorging may be achieved without freezing the neck, but does call for chilling of the bottles. The procedure requires a little practice, but is facilitated by the sediment being contained in the cavity of the hollow stopper. The muselet of the inverted bottle should be removed, care being taken to retain the stopper by gripping firmly; and as the bottle is brought up towards the vertical position the stopper is allowed to fly out. There will almost certainly be violent effervescence which should be arrested as quickly as possible. This is a simplified version of the classic method, *dégorgement à la volée.*

Where crown corks are used it is a good idea to partially release the closure by prizing up the flange gently, so that it may be released in one decisive attempt to provide a clean "blow-out."

---

* Supplier: *Triton Manufacturing Co., 15 North Avenue, London W.13.*

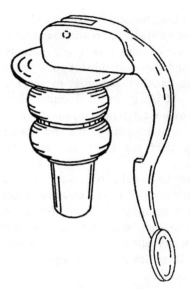

Triton bottle sealer

A small number of bottles may be treated one at a time and usually one ice tray will provide sufficient freezing mixture for the purpose; but for a large number a more elaborate rack and trough are needed. Needless to say, this will make considerable demands upon the ice supply, so additional trays would be required.

Before fitting the fresh stopper, the wine should be sniffed for soundness, any surplus sediment removed from the neck (with the handle of a teaspoon) and the bottle topped up. The use of the sealed polythene stopper, recommended for final bottling, will take care of most of the ullage. The wine will probably need a sweetening procedure, of which more anon.

The more ambitious winemaker, who processes 30 or more bottles at a time, may well prefer to use a more rapidly acting freezing mixture, such as solid CO_2* and methylated spirit. This mixture will provide a frozen slug quickly — in about 2 minutes — and enjoys a temperature near—70° C. (—94°F.), so the neck must be introduced very very slowly to avoid a fracture from the sudden thermal shock. Due to the intense cold an ice deposit will form inside the neck of the bottle, which is best removed by scraping with the handle of a teaspoon.

95

To prepare this coolant, the solid CO_2 should be broken up into small pieces and introduced gradually into a convenient volume of the spirit. A vigorous effervescence will take place initially, but as the spirit becomes cooler the activity will subside to a gentle bubbling action.

Solid CO_2 must be handled cautiously to avoid a "cold burn" as its temperature is near $-80°C.$ ($-112°F.$); either dispense it with tongs or handle it as quickly as hot cinders! To provide more economical use of the compound it is a good idea to lag the container with expanded polystyrene, ceiling tiles are ideal and are obtainable from most builders' merchants.

Some difficulty may be found in obtaining small quantities of the solid CO_2, as the manufacturers in this country generally *insist* upon a minimum order for a quantity of 25 lb. Fortunately, however, some commercial firms who use the compound, are frequently amenable to supplying amateur winemakers with small quantities. Alternatively, it might be obtained from ice-cream depots. 1 lb. should cope quite adequately with 30 bottles.

* D.C.L. Cardice.
* I.C.I. Drikold.

Adjusting Sweetness

All but the oldest of sparkling wines require a hint of sweetness; to provide a wider appeal for the white, or to enhance the character of some rosé and red sparkling wines, the supplement of a little sugar, or synthetic sweetening agent, is invariably desirable.

In the case of non-fermentable proprietary sweetening agents mostly based upon saccharin, such as "Liquid Sweetex", it is an attractive scheme to sweeten the dry basic wine (S.G. near .990) "to taste", *before* priming with sugar for the second (bottle) fermentation. Then this degree of sweetness should be produced in the finished wine. Individual bottles could of course be sweetened at disgorging.

Where the Clinitest method is used it is necessary to check for zero sugar first of all, sweeten the basic wine with artificial sweetener to taste and finally add the 2.4 oz. per gallon of priming sugar. This priming sugar will all be used up during the bottle fermentation, but the taste of the artificial sweetener will remain.

In the case of the "hydrometer method" it is also necessary to add, according to taste, the artificial sweetening agent initially, before the specific gravity is increased to 1.000 with granulated sugar or syrup. The presence of a small amount of the agent, at this stage, would have no appreciable effect upon the accuracy of the method.

The classic Champagne method is to add sugar contained in what is called a *liqueur d'expédition*. Our recommended *liqueur,* to provide a medium-sweet wine, is composed of equal volumes of 140 proof Polish spirit and 300 gravity syrup, then 30 ml. (1 fl. oz.) of this solution is cooled down to the same temperature as the wine and added carefully to each bottle, following disgorging; this minimises frothing. Needless to say, sufficient volume must be provided to accommodate the *liqueur;* some wine may need to be removed — but not wasted!

A 300 gravity syrup may be prepared by dissolving 2 lb. granulated sugar in 1 pint of water with the assistance of heat — care being taken not to "caramelise" the sugar by over-heating.

The inclusion of the spirit would indeed fortify the wine, but its real purpose is to prevent refermentation, which could be caused by traces of yeast still remaining. The occurrence of such a third fermentation would almost certainly build up an unsafe pressure level in the wired and stoppered bottles.

The degree of sweetness may be adjusted to suit the individual palate by varying the volume of the *liqueur*. Exact quantities may be found by experiment. Where a really sweet wine is preferred, this method is the most advisable; but for moderation in sweetness the synthetic "wine sweetener" is practically undetectable, as such, in our own experience.

To avoid the use of expensive duty-paid spirit the sugar may be stabilised by adding to each bottle 1.7 ml. of a 10% potassium sorbate solution (10 gm. in 100 ml.), dispensed from the graduated pipette as used for the acidity measurement. Such a solution may be prepared by dissolving 1 oz. of the compound in water, which is made up to 10 fl. oz. This solution would be useful also for stabilising other still wines, which are sweet and low in alcohol. It would be necessary to add a modicum of sulphite solution to avoid the dreaded 'geranium' odour!

Lactose, a non-fermentable (as far as wine yeasts are concerned) milk sugar, is used for sweetening some "stouts", but owing to the difficulty of dissolving this sugar, and its poor sweetening-power, we have abandoned the use; so cannot recommend it for sparkling wine.

The stoppering procedure would follow normal practice, but this time an enclosed polythene stopper should be used in place of the hollow one recommended for the second fermentation.

Only the purest of cane sugar is ever used to sweeten champagne. We have no doubt that a *champenoise* vintner would wring his hands and cry out with horror at some of our foregoing recommendations concerning synthetic sweeteners and potassium sorbate, but we feel that we have been successful with our own sparkling wine thus sweetened — despite the heresy.

CHAPTER 14

The Tank Method

The difficult skills of shaking down the yeast and disgorging, which are a central feature of the traditional champagne method, are unnecessary with the tank method. Production costs have been reduced by the perfection of this system and a bottle of sparkling wine is no longer an expensive luxury. Only those wine drinkers fortunate enough to have been reared on true champagne can detect the difference!

Briefly, the secondary fermentation is conducted in large vitreous enamelled lined tanks, or stainless steel tanks, designed to withstand considerable gas pressure and fitted with release valves set at predetermined pressures. Temperature can also be accurately controlled by heating and refrigerating coils, to give optimum fermentation conditions, later lowered to just above freezing point —4°C. (—25°F.) to facilitate clearing and precipitation of tartrates. When *attenuation* is satisfactory, and after a resting or settling period, the wine is filtered and bottled under pressure — any sugar or fortification adjustments having been made previously.

You may well ask what possible chance the amateur winemaker has of employing this process. The truth is that whilst he cannot copy the whole process he can certainly take advantage of some of its principles. Winemakers are past masters at the art of improvisation, and they may be interested to hear how we set out to solve this problem and produce our own tank fermentation apparatus.

Basic Equipment

1. A container that will safely withstand gas pressure of up to 100

lb. p.s.i. and readily adaptable to take a removable gas proof cover.

2. Dial reading pressure guage 0-100 p.s.i.

3. Adjustable pressure release valve, set at 65-70 p.s.i.

4. Draw-off valve fitted with siphon tube.

The choice of a suitable container is usually limited to one manufactured from stainless steel, thus ensuring sufficient strength to cope with maximum pressure of 100 p.s.i. Generally, containers made for other materials, particularly glass and earthenware, must be avoided; however, some plastic containers are adequately pressure rated to withstand 100 p.s.i.

The pressure gauge and release valve can be purchased either new or secondhand, from suppliers of spray painting equipment. Valves from the larger pressure cookers can be adapted. An adaptor plate should be substituted for the closure normally supplied and to this would be fitted a pressure gauge, relief valve and a delivery valve which is connected to a syphon tube extending almost to the base of the container. Recommended working pressure is 65-70 lb. p.s.i.

Containers made for pressurising home-made beer can also be used, but the pressure must be reduced to that recommended by the manufacturer, and not exceeded.

It is not practical for the amateur to fit refrigerating coils and freezing apparatus but we manage perfectly well by planning the secondary fermentation to be finished by November and leaving the wine under pressure until a really freezing spell of weather in January. The wine container is then exposed to the elements for a few days until the pressure gauge shows a considerable reduction. Alternatively, it can be put in a deep freeze or large refrigerator, and the required temperature can then be easily controlled.

All that remains is bottling.

Select and sterilise your champagne bottles as previously described, plug the necks with cotton wool and stand outside with the container to cool to the same low temperature. This simple procedure is essential as it helps to reduce loss of gas pressure in the next stage.

If your container is fitted with a tap, it is a good idea to fit a foot-length of rubber tube on to the tap so that it reaches the bottom of the bottle; the siphon tube can be adjusted in the same way. This allows the wine to flow in the bottle without undue splashing, which results in loss of gas pressure. The bottle should be filled to 1½ inches from the bottom of the stopper. This allows sufficient space (ullage) for expansion and gas pressure. Corks and stoppers are fitted immediately and wired down. Proper champagne wire muselets are best and not expensive to buy. Conventional racks are ideal but "do-it-yourself" enthusiasts will no doubt make their own.

The ideal storage conditions would be in a cool, even temperature of 12°C. (54°F.).

One advantage with this method of making sparkling wine is that it can be drawn off as "draught" and thus save the chore of bottling. If the pressure is initially raised and held at 70 lb. p.s.i. there is sufficient gas to serve all the wine, though the sparkle get less as the quantity reduces.

It is customary to proof-test pressurised vessels hydraulically to three times the working pressure i.e. 210 p.s.i. in this particular case. We would advise readers who propose to use this method to satisfy themselves that the vessel chosen is strong enough for the purpose, and that there is a safety margin.

Carbonated Wine

In addition to the procedure from the *cuve close,* or tank method, a good deal of commercial sparkling wine and other similar beverages are made by the simple carbonation of wine or fermented fruit bases. This is generally achieved by chilling the wine which has been partially de-aerated by vacuum, at just above its freezing-point, and then by impregnating it with carbon dioxide gas under pressure. In order to provide a satisfactory sparkle it is important to admit the gas very slowly.

Sparkling wine made this way will not have the good bubble retention of one originating from the champagne or tank methods. The persistent running bead associated with these methods is due to the formation of an unstable chemical compound called ethyl pyrocarbonate which decomposes slowly on releasing the pressure into ethyl alcohol and carbon dioxide gas, so continues to reinforce that gas which is dissolved physically in the wine.

Owing to the relatively short processing duration of the tank method the gas retention is not quite as good as for the bottle fermented wine — not so much ethyl pyrocarbonate is formed. But it is certainly better than straight carbonated wine, which loses its sparkle quite quickly despite the initial foaming effervescence and frequently lacks a persistent bouquet. Nevertheless a carbonated wine does provide a refreshing effervescent beverage to be enjoyed on a hot summer's day, or at any other time for that matter.

As amateurs we can quite easily make our own almost "instant" sparkling wine by using a sparklet siphon. Choose any delicate wine (it may be sweet or dry) and fill the siphon which should be chilled in a refrigerator to near freezing point, but avoid actually freezing the wine, then introduce the carbon dioxide gas from a Sparklet bulb as slowly as possible. This is facilitated by only a partial puncture of the cap, so that the gas escapes at the minimum rate and this may be achieved by very careful tightening of the bulb retainer, but this is usually difficult to accomplish in practice.

The siphon is then shaken up to be returned to the refrigerator and the thermostat readjusted to the normal setting, so allowing the wine to recover, as it would then be too cold to appreciate on serving. Before dispensing, the siphon should be inverted and the excess gas allowed to escape by releasing the lever. On removing the head, the wine may be decanted into glasses, and providing this is done out of sight, it is surprising how many of the guests may be deceived by the attractive freshness of the sparkling wine so produced.

MALO-LACTIC FERMENTATION. Certain commercial wines, notably Mateus rosé and vinho verde, are said to derive their pétillant sparkle from what is called a malo-lactic fermentation.

This malo-lactic fermentation sometimes happens (it is difficult, but not impossible, to encourage deliberately) when the appropriate bacteria is present under warm conditions and then it acts upon the malic acid present in the wine. The malic acid is partially converted into lactic acid with the evolution of carbon dioxide gas which provides an attractive sparkle. Lactic acid is less active on the palate, so the effective acidity is reduced, and as mentioned in Chapter 2, such a happening is welcomed with a poor year in the Champagne. However a malo-lactic fermentation should not be considered as a reliable means of making a semi-sparkling wine. It must be regarded mainly as of academic interest

102

in this respect and will not function in the presence of an excess of sulphite. When excess sugar is present an off-flavour may very well develop.

The tendency for wines made from certain ingredients to develop a natural sparkle has been observed by country winemakers for many years. The ingredients concerned frequently included: gooseberry, rhubarb and apple. But, it is was not until recent years that the reason was appreciated—all three are rich in malic acid and, before the now popular incorporation of sulphite (Campden tablets), the wines frequently became pétillant (semi-sparkling). This was not always intentional and can, in fact, still occur with relatively low concentrations of sulphite.

CHAPTER 15

Tasting and Serving Sparkling Wine

Having succeeded in making this somewhat exacting but delectable wine, and resisted the temptation to drink it prematurely, thoughts of throwing a party to celebrate the occasion naturally spring to mind. Before rushing to send out invitations (and please don't forget us!) we strongly advise you to open a bottle well in advance to test gas pressure, clarity and quality. This advice is offered to save you from a nightmare experience that happened to a rather over-confident winemaker friend of ours at his first sparkling wine party. His guests, chosen for their expert knowledge of sparkling wine, gathered around him with champagne glasses at the ready, eagerly watching and waiting for the familiar "Pop". The wire muselet was removed and cork gently eased. Nothing happened! A second more determined twist and pull, still nothing happened! Eventually, after a few more unsuccessful attempts one of the guests, dying for a drink, produced a corkscrew and with great humiliation the damned cork was drawn. To cap it all, not one little bubble had the courtesy to rise up and save the day. Not that there's anything wrong with a bottle of chilled still gooseberry wine.....

Knowing that this calamity couldn't possibly happen to one of our readers, here are a few tips to ensure a successful tasting.

First chill your wines in either the refrigerator or an ice bucket. This has two important effects; pressure is reduced considerably making opening less hazardous and serving easier, and the running bead of gas is retained for a longer period. Moreover, a chilled wine is more acceptable and refreshing to the palate. It is equally important not to *over*-chill sparkling wine, for if it is drunk very cold the gas is quickly released by the warmth of the stomach, one feels blown out and the too familiar burping sounds follow! A half-hour in the refrigerator, in the milk section, is sufficient time, but allow a little longer if you use an ice-bucket.

It may seem a slight to the reader's intelligence to explain how to open a bottle of sparkling wine but, like most things, there is a right and wrong way. To add an air of gaiety to a celebration it is common practice to let the cork or stopper "fly" and the wine gush out. At the risk of being spoilsports, this is the wrong way to open sparkling wine. A released cork with somewhere in the region of 50 p.s.i. behind it can be dangerous should it strike anyone in the face (this occurred at the National Wine Festival in 1971 when a steward was hit in the mouth by a stopper that flew immediately the wire was removed). So always cover the stopper with a napkin, holding it on tight, and pointing it away from you and the guests, as you untwist or cut the wire hood. Then allow the pressure to push against your hand as you ease the stopper gently out. Should the wine be very lively the napkin will also prevent the wine gushing out over everybody before you get it into the glasses. Never try to control a gushing wine by putting your thumb or the palm of your hand over it, unless of course you don't mind getting an eyeful.

Opinions differ as to the best type of champagne glass to use. The tall tulip or flute glasses have the advantage that they show off the sparkle and colour to the best advantage, the bouquet is funnelled to the nose and the dancing beads seem to run longer. For those who prefer a less effervescent wine for drinking, the now unpopular saucer type glass is best as the large surface area allows the gas to escape quicker. As a bonus this type of glass can be stacked up to six glasses high and the wine poured into the top glass and allow to cascade all the way down filling each glass in turn. Connoisseurs may frown but this makes an amusing party piece! There are other types of glasses, of course, but these two shapes have proved the most popular.

Avoid over-filling glasses: it is most irritating precariously balancing a champagne glass filled to the brim whilst waiting for a toast to be given. When washing glasses avoid using detergents as the slightest trace left in the glass can reduce the gay effect of the running bead.

FLUTE

TULIP

COUPE

Glasses for sparkling wine

Show Competitions

There is nothing like competitions to improve standards, and that has proved the case with our hobby. At local and National shows, individual winemakers do battle for humble yet coveted awards and are given careful and impartial criticism of the wines by qualified judges.

If you are thinking of exhibiting your sparkling wine, firstly send for the schedule of the show in which you are interested; a copy of the Amateur Winemakers' National Guild of Judges handbook would also be invaluable.

Next, assess your wine carefully to meet the Show schedule standards. This may seem elementary but it is easy to make the common mistake of entering the wine in the wrong class. Winemakers often find difficulty in being completely impartial when judging their own wine and we recommend that you seek the opinion of a fellow winemaker known to have a discerning palate and preferably knowledgeable about sparkling wine.

106

Your wine will be judged for presentation (2 points), clarity and colour (4 points), sediment (4 points), effervescence (10 points), bouquet (10 points), flavour and balance (20 points). Total 50 points.

Presentation Covers:

1. Correct type of bottle
2. Correct type of cork or stopper
3. Correct size and position of label or labels and description of wine.

} These details will be shown on the show schedule

4. Bottle must be clean inside, and outside.
5. Cork or stopper must be clean (not necessarily new).
6. Bottle must be filled (for sparkling wine) so that there is 1½ inch air space between top of wine and bottom of cork.

Under the heading of *colour and clarity* a maximum of four points is given for star bright wine free from haze and floaters, etc. Deduction is made for any faults depending upon severity, and one point can be awarded for good colour according to type of wine.

It is quality rather than pungency that we seek when judging the bouquet of a wine — elegant subtle volatile esters delight the the nose and excite the senses in anticipation of the pleasure to follow.

To help you assess your own wine impartially the following procedure is advocated.

Sparkling Wine

1. Half fill a tulip shaped champagne glass and allow the first violent effervescence to subside; "nose" the wine and inhale slow, long and steadily.
2. Don't concentrate too hard upon trying to identify the ingredients, but assess the aromatic freshness, and whether it invites you to drink the wine.
3. Award ten points if it is outstanding in this respect and deduct points accordingly for any foreign smell, oxidation, etc.

Acetification is easily identified by its vinegary smell. Should you be unfortunate enough to find *this* in your wine it is pointless to exhibit it regardless of whatever other merits it may have. Save it for salad dressing! The final tasting and quality assessment carries 20 points and is the most important part of wine tasting.

1. Having assessed the bouquet and made your judgement, the same glass of wine is used for the tasting.
2. Take a good quantity of wine into your mouth (not a tiny sip) and slowly chew it; at the same time incline your head slightly downwards, part your lips slightly and draw air through and over the wine. This takes practice but is soon mastered. This aids in judging the aroma and esters. Concentrate and decide if the wine is correct to class (dry, sweet, etc.). If it is not to class there is no point in judging its further qualities. If it is correct to class in this respect, does it meet the other requirements for its type, balance of acid, tannin, body, sugar and alcohol?

Remind yourself constantly of the class definition as laid down in the show schedule. The flavour should be free from imperfections, oxidation, off-flavours mustiness, etc. Try at all times to avoid personal preference — judges are expected to be impartial and able to evaluate merit in any type of wine regardless of whether or not it would be a wine of their own choice. First tastings are relatively easy as it is not all that difficult to distinguish between low and high quality wines. It is in the final adjudication of wines of relatively equal merit that the skill and discriminating palate of the judge is truly tested.

Having judged your own wine on this standard and marked your sheet accordingly, compare it with your friends' marking and see how it fares. Don't be hypercritical (very few wines are perfect even in the commercial world) so providing it is within striking distance of the following qualities put a bottle or two into the next show.

1. The wine, cork, bottle and label must comply with show schedule requirements.
2. Bottle sound and clean inside and out and filled to the stated level.
3. The wine must be bright and free from floaters and deposits. If your wine has thrown down a slight yeast or tartrate deposit this will have to remain and you will lose a point or two. In still wines these could be racked off but obviously not in a sparkling wine.

4. When uncorked the pressure should not be too high, resulting in the wine gushing out in an uncontrollable fountain.
5. When poured the bead (bubble) should be lively and small, running continously, the opposite to the familiarly known carbonated lemonade bubble which is large and disappears after a few seconds.
6. The bouquet should be clean fresh and inviting.
7. Taste should be delicate and leave the palate clean, light in body but not thin, a subtle difference.

In the authors' experience in judging sparkling wines the most common faults found are:
1. Loss of gas pressure through faulty stoppers or corks, resulting in poor if any, sparkle.
2. A lack of zest and too low an acidity.
3. Flavour out of character and too dominant.
4. Wines not star-bright.
5. Yeasty flavour and deposits.

The reader will by now appreciate the difficulties in exhibiting a first class bottle of sparkling wine. He should also be rightly proud of his skill if he can attain perfection; exhibiting still wines is child's play in comparison!

Measurement of Acidity

Apparatus required:
   One 10 ml. graduated pipette (burette)
   One 5 ml. pipette
   One 100 ml. conical flask
Chemical solutions required:
   Decinormal (N/10) sodium hydroxide solution
   Distilled water
   Indicator solution 1% phenolphthalein

Method:

A representative sample of the wine or must should be "sucked-up" into the 5 ml. pipette to just above the fine calibrated ring and be allowed to run away to waste in order to cleanse the pipette. The procedure is then repeated, when the index finger (preferably dry) is quickly placed over the end of the pipette and the pressure released slightly to allow the falling level to coincide with the calibrated ring. Dryness of the finger, a dodge familiar to analytical chemists, provides a much better control in adjusting the level of the liquid in either the pipette or graduated pipette.

The wine contained in the pipette is then run into a clean 100 ml. conical flask and when empty, is allowed to drain for approximately 20 seconds. Some 30 ml. of distilled water is poured into the flask, and should be used to wash in any wine attached to the neck. To settle the query, which must be running through many minds, the addition of water may dilute the acid in the wine, but in no way does it affect the total quantity present, and it is this that we are measuring.

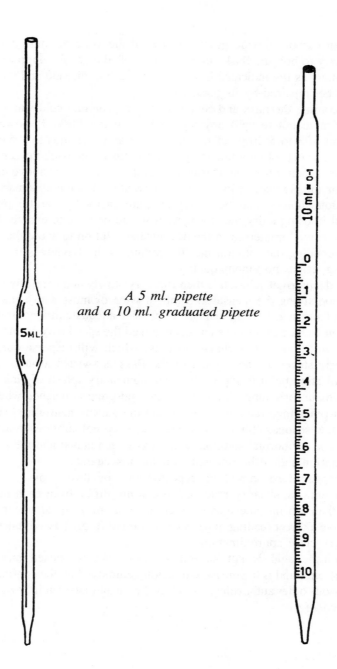

A 5 ml. pipette
and a 10 ml. graduated pipette

When carbon dioxide gas is present in the wine or must it will be necessary to boil the flask gently to drive off the gas for approximately 2 minutes, as the indicator is sensitive to carbon dioxide and its action would be impaired by its presence.

On cooling the flask and contents, under a running cold-water tap, it is advisable not to spill any tap water into the flask. Following the addition of 3 to 5 drops of the indicator it now remains to "suck-up" the decinormal solution into the graduated pipette in much the same way as before, then, following rinsing the level is taken to just above the zero mark on the graduated pipette and is allowed to fall on to this mark. This operation should soon be mastered quite easily by careful pressure control in using a dry index-finger. It would be wise to ensure that the burette is well immersed in the decinormal solution to avoid the danger of introducing the solution into the mouth as the flavour is not wildly exciting, it has no vinous quality!

The decinormal solution is then run very slowly and carefully into the flask containing the measured 5 ml. of wine or must with agitation of the contents in a swirling manner, to provide adequate mixing of the two solutions. Once experience has been gained the speed may be increased. There will be a colour change to pink, which will disperse quickly in the early stages as the content of the flask is swirled around. As the neutralisation point is approached the momentary splash of pink colour will remain for a longer period, but the end-point is reached when only a faint pink tinge remains constant throughout the neutralised solution for a few seconds. Should a permanent, deep colouration be achieved too much decinormal solution would have been added and the result of the titration should be rejected as being inaccuarate.

The procedure should be repeated two or three times to obtain agreement. Satisfactory readings should not differ from each other by more than 0.5 ml. and then an average value may be calculated which will give a direct reading in parts per thousand (p.p.t.) as sulphuric acid, for very close approximation.

Sulphuric acid is not natural to wine, but is chosen purely for convenience and is the measure of acidity employed on the continent and by various other authorities, including Acton and Duncan in *Progressive Winemaking*.

Example:
    1st reading   4.7 ml.

112

2nd reading   4.3 ml.
3rd reading   4.8 ml.

$$\text{Mean reading} \frac{13.8}{3} = 4.6 \text{ ml. or } 4.6 \text{ p.p.t. of acid}$$

A base for sparkling wine should return an acidity of 4 p.p.t. but this would be expected to fall slightly during maturation. Some readers may prefer to work at a lower value of acidity, possibly nearer to 3 p.p.t. to be in keeping with sparkling wine from a warmer climate than experienced in the Champagne area. To convert p.p.t. in sulphuric to p.p.t. in tartaric multiply by 1.53.

TABLE 3

CORRESPONDING ACIDITIES IN PARTS PER THOUSAND
OF VARIOUS ACIDS

Sulphuric Acid	Citric Acid	Malic Acid	Tartaric Acid
0.5	0.72	0.69	0.77
1.0	1.43	1.37	1.53
1.5	2.14	2.03	2.29
2.0	2.86	2.74	3.06
2.5	3.58	3.42	3.83
3.0	4.29	4.10	4.59
3.5	5.01	4.78	5.36
4.0	5.72	5.47	6.12
4.5	6.44	6.15	6.89
5.0	7.15	6.84	7.65
5.5	7.87	7.52	8.42
6.0	8.58	8.21	9.19
6.5	9.30	8.89	9.96
7.0	10.0	9.58	10.7
7.5	10.7	10.3	11.5
8.0	11.4	10.9	12.2
8.5	12.1	11.6	13.0
9.0	12.9	12.3	13.8
9.5	13.6	13.0	14.6
10.0	14.3	13.7	15.3

When the acidity of red wines is being determined some difficulty will certainly be encountered in determining the correct end-point and here it would be advisable to add 50 ml. of distilled water to provide greater dilution. The pigments in the wine act as an indicator themselves and some experience will be required to recognise the true end-point, but as the colouration of the musts or wines for sparkling bases are not expected to be dense we would not anticipate undue difficulty in this respect.

Many suppliers market moderately priced acid testing kits which feature simplified apparatus. They are not necessarily quite so accurate as the laboratory equipment we describe, but the method is based upon exactly the same principle, and some readers may prefer what might be considered as a simplified approach.

TABLE 4

WEIGHTS OF VARIOUS ACIDS IN
OUNCES PER GALLON REQUIRED TO PROVIDE A GIVEN
ACIDITY IN P.P.T. AS SULPHURIC ACID

Weight of Acid ozs./gal.	Citric Acid	Malic Acid	Tartaric Acid
⅛	0.54	0.57	0.51
¼	1.09	1.14	1.02
⅜	1.63	1.71	1.53
½	2.19	2.28	2.04
⅝	2.73	2.85	2.55
¾	3.29	3.42	3.04
⅞	3.83	3.99	3.57
1	4.37	4.56	4.07
1⅛	4.91	5.13	4.58
1¼	5.66	5.70	5.09
1⅜	6.00	6.27	5.60
1½	6.56	6.84	6.11
1⅝	7.10	7.41	6.62
1¾	7.66	7.98	7.13
1⅞	8.20	8.55	7.64
2	8.73	9.12	8.15

May we again stress the need to measure the acidity of all musts (most acid inclusions in recipes can only be regarded as a guide), as many winemakers appear to experience difficulty in assessing the correct acid balance flavour wise.

The apparatus and solutions should be obtainable from laboratory or the more specialised winemaker's supplier and should not prove to be unduly expensive. Incidentally, the decinormal solution should be stored in small well stoppered bottles and it should be pointed out that the solution does not have an unlimited shelf-life, especially with a large air space in the bottle.

Readers who experience difficulty in obtaining decinormal sodium hydroxide soluion could well take advantage of the acid testing solution currently available from Boots the Chemist. This is labelled .2M sodium hydroxide solution and is twice the strength of our original recommendation, which means that either you will need to double the reading of the graduated pipette, or use two pipettefuls of the wine when the reading will be normal.

INDEX

INDEX

INDEX

INDEX

INDEX

Also available from Nexus Special Interests Books

Brewing Beers Like Those You Buy *David Line*
First Steps in Winemaking *C.J.J. Berry*
Home Brewed Beers & Stouts *C.J.J. Berry*
Making Wines Like Those You Buy *Bryan Acton & Peter Duncan*
130 New Winemaking Recipes *C.J.J. Berry*
Winemaking with Concentrates *Peter Duncan*